Kindness Costs N
Pricel

Surendra Shrivastava

Kindness Costs Nothing, Yet It's Priceless

Surendra Shrivastava

Published by Surendra Shrivastava, 2024.

While every precaution has been taken in the preparation of this book, the publisher assumes no responsibility for errors or omissions, or for damages resulting from the use of the information contained herein.

KINDNESS COSTS NOTHING, YET IT'S PRICELESS

First edition. October 7, 2024.

ISBN: 979-8227864000

Written by Surendra Shrivastava.

Surendra Shrivastava
(Self-Help Author)

TABLE of Contents

CHAPTER 1 2

The Ripple Effect of a Kind Gesture 3
How Small Acts of Kindness Transform Lives 4
Paying It Forward: The Chain Reaction of Compassion 5
The Unexpected Rewards of Being Kind

CHAPTER 2 2

Kindness as a Superpower 3
Why Empathy is a Strength, Not a Weakness 4
From Bullied to Beloved: How Kindness Changes Narratives
Turning Challenges into Opportunities for Kindness

CHAPTER 3 2

The Science Behind Kindness 3
How Acts of Kindness Boost Mental Health 4
The Biology of a Kind Heart: How Our Brain Reacts to Kindness 5
Kindness and Longevity: The Secret to a Happy Life

CHAPTER 4 2

Everyday Kindness: Small Actions, Big Impact 3
How to Practice Kindness Even When Life Gets Tough 4
Random Acts of Kindness: Ideas for Everyday Life 5
Building a Habit of Kindness: Making it a Lifestyle

CHAPTER 5 2

Kindness in a Digital World 3
Spreading Positivity Online: How to Be a Digital Role Model 4
Dealing with Negativity and Hate: Responding with Kindness
Building an Online Community Rooted in Kindness

From the Author

DEDICATION

This book is dedicated to those who have journeyed with me through the landscapes of the heart and the mind. Your presence, encouragement, and love have been the guiding light in my creative process.

To my parents,

Your unwavering support and boundless love have provided the foundation upon which I stand. You have instilled in me the values of hard work, resilience, and the beauty of simplicity. This collection is as much yours as it is mine.

To my siblings,

You have been my first friends and lifelong companions. Your laughter, kindness, and shared memories are woven into the fabric of these poems.

To my friends,

Thank you for being my sounding board, my critics, and my cheerleaders. Your insights, whether gentle or tough, have helped shape my work into what it is today.

CHAPTER ONE

The Ripple Effect of a Kind Gesture

How Small Acts of Kindness Transform Lives

Imagine this: You're at your local coffee shop, waiting in line, just another ordinary day. The line is moving slowly, and you can sense the tension in the air—people checking their watches, scrolling through their phones, caught up in their own worlds. As you reach the counter, you notice the barista's tired smile and decide to do something a little different. "Add the next person's coffee to my bill," you say with a wink. The barista's eyebrows rise, and a genuine smile brightens her face.

The person behind you, a middle-aged man who looks like he's had a long day, is visibly surprised when the barista informs him that his coffee has already been paid for. He glances around to find you, but you've already walked away, not expecting anything in return. But that small act—a few extra dollars—has set a ripple in motion. It's not just about the coffee; it's about the gesture, the unexpected warmth, the reminder that sometimes, people are kind simply because they can be.

The man takes his coffee with a lighter heart, a little more optimistic than before. He calls his daughter later that evening, something he hasn't done in weeks, and ends up spending an hour chatting with her about everything under the sun. That simple act of buying a coffee has turned his day around, and in turn, he's managed to brighten someone else's. And so, the ripple moves forward.

It's in these seemingly insignificant actions that the true magic of kindness lies. We often underestimate how far a smile, a kind word, or a small gesture can travel. It's not always about grand, life-changing moments. Sometimes, it's about how you made someone feel in a fleeting instant, and how that feeling spreads to others like concentric circles on water.

A study once found that when we witness acts of kindness, it activates the release of serotonin and dopamine—chemicals associated with feelings of happiness and well-being. Not only does the person receiving the kindness feel good, but the one who witnesses it also experiences a boost. It's as though our brains are wired to respond to kindness with a sense of connection and gratitude. This makes kindness contagious, a spark that lights up a chain of positivity, one person at a time.

Now, think of the power in this: a small act of kindness can shift someone's mindset, soften their stress, and perhaps, give them the push they need to be kind to someone else. It's the idea that your kindness, no matter how small, is never wasted. It may fade from your memory, but its impact can last far longer than you imagine.

Paying It Forward: The Chain Reaction of Compassion

One of the most beautiful aspects of kindness is its ability to inspire others to act in kind. There's a famous story about a diner in a small town, where a woman, feeling generous, decided to pay for the meal of the couple sitting across from her. She did this quietly, without fanfare, simply leaving a note that read, "Have a wonderful day, and pay it forward."

The couple, surprised and touched, left the diner with smiles on their faces. On their way home, they stopped at a grocery store, and there, they encountered a single mother struggling with her groceries, trying to balance her toddler on one hip. They offered to help, paid for a few of her items, and wished her a great day. The mother, overwhelmed by their generosity, went home that night with a renewed sense of hope. She baked cookies with her child and decided to share them with her elderly neighbor who lived alone.

The elderly neighbor, who often spent his days in solitude, was delighted by the unexpected visit. He told her stories of his younger days, and as they talked, he realized he had a surplus of vegetables in his garden. The next morning, he packed a basket full of fresh produce and left it on the porch of the local church, knowing it would find its way to families in need.

Each act in this chain might seem small on its own—just a meal, a few groceries, some cookies, a basket of vegetables. Yet, together, they weave a tapestry of connection, a series of moments that might never have happened had one person not taken the first step.

This is the true essence of "paying it forward." It's a quiet revolution, where one person's choice to be kind becomes the spark that ignites kindness in others. It's the idea that you might not be able to change the whole world, but you can change someone's world, even if just for a moment. And in doing so, you plant a seed of kindness that may grow in ways you'll never witness.

Think about it—when was the last time someone did something unexpectedly kind for you? How did it make you feel? Did it inspire you to smile a little more at strangers, to be more patient with your family, to reach out to an old friend? And how might those actions have impacted those around you?

Sometimes, the simplest gestures have the power to create a chain reaction that moves through communities, touching lives we may never meet. It's a reminder that even when we feel small, even when we feel like our actions won't make a difference, we have the power to start a wave of change. Kindness is like a pebble dropped in a pond—its ripples extend far beyond what we can see.

The Unexpected Rewards of Being Kind

What's in it for you? It's a question we often ask ourselves, consciously or unconsciously. And while the beauty of kindness lies in giving without expecting, there's no denying that being kind often rewards us in surprising ways. These rewards aren't always tangible—more often, they are felt deeply, in the quiet satisfaction of knowing you've made someone's day a little better.

When you help someone in need, you might notice a shift within yourself—a lightness that wasn't there before, a sense of purpose that lingers long after the moment has passed. Kindness has a way of connecting us to our own humanity, to the parts of us that yearn for connection and community. In a world that can sometimes feel cold and indifferent, being kind can be a small rebellion, a way of saying, "I see you, and you matter."

Many people who volunteer regularly speak about the "helper's high," a term coined to describe the rush of endorphins that comes from doing something good for someone else. This isn't just an emotional experience; it's backed by science. Research has shown that performing acts of kindness triggers the release of oxytocin, sometimes called the "love hormone," which makes us feel closer to others and even has physical benefits like lowering blood pressure.

But beyond the science, there's something deeply personal about the rewards of kindness. It's in the way a stranger's gratitude lingers in your mind long after the interaction has ended, or how a child's laughter makes you feel like you've added a little more light to the world. It's in the unexpected friendships that blossom when you reach out to someone who seems lonely, and the warmth you feel when you see the smile you've brought to someone's face.

Imagine a world where these small, everyday kindnesses were the norm rather than the exception. Where we held the door for each other, shared a meal without counting the cost, and offered a listening ear to those who needed it. A world where we recognized that in giving to others, we are also giving to ourselves—a sense of connection, of belonging, of knowing that we are all in this together.

Kindness, after all, costs nothing, but its value is immeasurable. It is a currency that enriches both the giver and the receiver, creating bonds that can last a lifetime or just a fleeting moment, but always leaving a mark. And it starts with the simplest of choices—one that you make every day when you decide how you want to move through the world.

As we dive deeper into the essence of kindness, let's consider the often-overlooked moments, the quiet acts that don't make headlines but can change the trajectory of a day—or even a life. We tend to think of kindness in grand gestures, in stories of people raising thousands of dollars for charity or dedicating their lives to service. But real, everyday kindness is much simpler than that. It's a gentle word, a nod of understanding, a reassuring smile at a stranger who looks lost.

Kindness is universal. It doesn't matter where you come from, your background, or your beliefs—kindness is a language that everyone understands. Picture a busy subway in a city like New York, where people from all walks of life are moving through their routines. The atmosphere is typically hurried, impersonal. But then, an elderly woman struggles with her bags. Without thinking twice, a young man steps forward, lifts her bags, and helps her to her seat. She doesn't speak much English, and he doesn't know her language, but they exchange smiles—something unspoken but deeply understood passes between them.

In a matter of seconds, the energy in the subway car changes. Others who had been glued to their phones look up and take notice. Some smile, and you can see the invisible shift in their faces—a reminder that maybe, just maybe, they could do something kind today too. They won't all go out and perform a grand gesture, but perhaps they'll smile at their colleagues or hold the door for someone who looks like they're having a tough day. This moment of kindness has moved from one person to many, like ripples spreading out from a single pebble dropped into water.

And yet, even though kindness is universal, it's also incredibly personal. It has a unique power to connect us to others, but also to connect us to ourselves. It's in those quiet moments of reflection, when you think back to a kind word someone offered you during a tough time, or a gesture that seemed small but meant the world. Sometimes, it's a simple message from a friend saying, "I'm thinking of you," or a neighbor bringing over soup when you're feeling under the weather.

Think back to a time when you were at your lowest—when it felt like the weight of the world was resting on your shoulders. Perhaps it was during a time of loss, uncertainty, or when you were struggling to find your footing. Now, imagine how different that experience might have been if, during that time, a stranger had taken a moment to notice you, to offer a word of encouragement, or to simply acknowledge your existence in a crowded world. That's the thing about kindness—it doesn't erase our struggles, but it can lighten the burden, even if just for a moment.

The Invisibility of Kindness: When You Don't See the Impact

One of the most challenging aspects of kindness is that you don't always see its impact. Unlike a job where you see the results of your work, or a project where you get feedback, acts of kindness often disappear into the ether, leaving you wondering if they made any difference at all. But what we need to remember is that not all impacts are visible, and not all rewards are immediate.

Consider the story of a teacher who, every day, wrote a small positive note to a different student in her class. She never expected anything in return—she simply wanted to brighten a child's day. Years later, at a class reunion, a grown-up student approached her, holding a crumpled piece of paper. It was one of her notes from years ago, which he had kept in his wallet through the toughest times in his life. That little piece of paper, scribbled with a simple "I believe in you," had been a beacon of hope when he felt lost and alone.

Not every act of kindness comes back to you in such a clear way, and that can be disheartening. It's human nature to want acknowledgment, to want to see the fruits of our efforts. But kindness teaches us a different lesson: sometimes, the greatest impacts are the ones we never know about. It's like planting seeds in a garden you may never see grow. You don't plant because you expect to harvest the flowers; you plant because it's the right thing to do.

For every story we hear about kindness coming full circle, there are countless others that go unnoticed. The cup of coffee bought for a stranger, the compliment given to someone feeling insecure, the encouragement shared with someone who is struggling—these acts often fade into the background of our busy lives, but their echoes remain in the hearts of those who receive them.

This invisibility doesn't make kindness any less powerful. It makes it purer. It means that when you choose to be kind, you're doing so without an agenda, without an expectation of return. You are contributing to a world that is just a little bit softer, a little bit more understanding. And while you may never know the full extent of what your kindness has achieved, you can rest assured that it has created a ripple somewhere, in some corner of the world.

Kindness as a Form of Strength: Overcoming Cynicism

In a world that often feels driven by self-interest, where success is measured by what you can gain rather than what you can give, choosing kindness can feel like an act of defiance. It's easy to become cynical, to believe that the world is a harsh place where nice people finish last. But those who embrace kindness know a different truth: that kindness is a form of strength, not weakness.

It takes courage to be kind when it's not reciprocated, to offer understanding when faced with rudeness, to give without expecting anything in return. It requires inner strength to smile at someone who scowls, to listen patiently when someone is venting, and to remain compassionate even when the world seems to have little compassion to offer. Yet, this is exactly why kindness matters—because it is a choice, a choice that says, "I refuse to let the negativity of the world change who I am."

Kindness doesn't mean letting others walk all over you; it doesn't mean being a pushover. It means choosing to remain open-hearted, even when experience tells you to close off. It means recognizing that everyone is fighting their own battles, even the person who cuts you off in traffic or the colleague who snaps at you during a meeting. It means understanding that people are not always their best selves, but that doesn't mean they are beyond reach.

Take the story of a woman who worked as a cashier at a supermarket. Every day, she made a point to greet each customer with a smile, to compliment them on something small—their outfit, their choice of fruit, the way they interacted with their kids. Many people brushed her off or mumbled a distracted "thanks." But one day, a man came through her line and paused, tears welling in his eyes. He told her that her smile was the first kind thing anyone had done for him in weeks. He had been contemplating ending his life, but her simple kindness made him feel seen, made him believe that maybe, just maybe, life was worth living after all.

That woman may have thought her greetings were insignificant, just part of her job, a way to pass the time. But in that moment, she understood that kindness is not just about the gesture itself; it's about the potential it holds to change the course of someone's life, to turn someone away from the brink. Her strength, her decision to remain kind despite everything, became a lifeline for a stranger.

We often think of strength as something visible—muscles, power, control. But sometimes, strength is quiet. It's the ability to keep extending kindness in a world that doesn't always reward it. It's the willingness to reach out to others even when you're tired, even when you're hurting. It's the persistence to believe in the goodness of people, even when that goodness is hard to find.

And here lies the paradox of kindness: while it may feel like it costs us something—time, energy, vulnerability—it also replenishes us. It fills us up in ways that nothing else can, because in being kind, we are aligning ourselves with a deeper truth: that we are all connected, that every person we encounter is an opportunity to make the world a little better, a little kinder.

As we journey further into the intricacies of kindness, it's essential to acknowledge the inner struggle many of us face when deciding whether or not to extend a kind gesture. It's a mental tug-of-war between self-preservation and empathy, between conserving our own energy and extending it to others. Have you ever been in a situation where you hesitated to reach out to someone who seemed troubled, worried that your effort might not be appreciated or that you might be rejected? That hesitation is a familiar feeling. It's the fear of vulnerability, the fear that our kindness might be misunderstood or even rebuffed.

Yet, it's precisely this vulnerability that makes acts of kindness so powerful. When you choose to be kind, you're stepping out of your comfort zone and offering a piece of yourself to someone else. It's a reminder that humanity is built not on rigid walls of self-interest but on bridges of understanding and compassion. And every time you cross that bridge, you make it easier for others to follow. Kindness becomes a path that others can walk too—a way to reconnect with the better parts of themselves.

The Science Behind Kindness: How It Transforms Us Physically and Mentally

But kindness isn't just about warm feelings and spiritual fulfillment. There's actual science behind how kindness impacts our bodies and minds. Studies have shown that engaging in acts of kindness releases oxytocin, the "love hormone," which helps reduce blood pressure and improves overall heart health. This is why many scientists refer to oxytocin as the "cardioprotective hormone." It's fascinating to think that something as simple as holding the door for someone or complimenting a stranger could physically strengthen your heart, literally and metaphorically.

This physiological response doesn't just benefit the person performing the act of kindness—it also extends to those who witness it. Imagine you're in a coffee shop, waiting for your morning espresso, when you see a customer pay for the coffee of the person behind them. You don't know either of them, and you're not directly involved, but you feel a warmth spread through you. This is called "elevation," a psychological phenomenon where witnessing acts of kindness inspires you and makes you feel more connected to humanity. It's like a surge of positive energy that makes you want to go out and do something kind yourself.

The transformative effects of kindness go even deeper when it comes to mental health. For those struggling with anxiety or depression, one of the hardest things can be the feeling of isolation, of being cut off from the rest of the world. Acts of kindness, even small ones, can be a powerful way to bridge that gap. It shifts the focus outward, helping people feel less trapped within their own thoughts and more connected to others. It's why therapists often encourage their patients to volunteer or engage in community service—because the act of giving can be a balm for a weary heart.

Think about the last time you were feeling low, and you did something nice for someone else, even if it was as simple as sending an encouraging text to a friend. In that moment, the weight of your own worries might have felt just a little bit lighter. Kindness has that effect—it's a subtle but profound shift in perspective, a reminder that we are not alone in our struggles.

Kindness in the Digital Age: The Power of Positive Online Interactions

In today's world, where so much of our interaction takes place online, kindness has taken on new forms. We often hear about the negative aspects of social media—the trolling, the divisive comments, the isolation that can come from endless scrolling. But social media also has the potential to be a powerful platform for spreading kindness, if we choose to use it that way.

A single positive comment can turn around someone's day. Think about a time when you posted something—maybe it was a photo you were proud of, a vulnerable thought, or an update on something you were struggling with. And then someone, maybe even someone you didn't know well, left a kind comment. It probably wasn't anything grand—just a simple "You've got this!" or "This is awesome!"—but in that moment, it felt like a lifeline. It's a reminder that even in the vast, often anonymous digital world, we have the power to reach out and touch someone's life.

This kind of online kindness can be particularly impactful for people who feel isolated in their real-life communities. It can be a way to connect with like-minded individuals, to find support networks, and to remind ourselves that there are people out there who understand us, even if we've never met them in person. For many, a supportive online community can be the difference between feeling completely alone and feeling like they belong.

But kindness online requires intentionality. It's easy to get caught up in the rush of notifications, the constant stream of new content. Being kind in the digital space means pausing, taking a moment to consider how your words might affect someone else, and choosing to spread positivity instead of adding to the noise. It means reaching out to someone who might seem distant, sending a quick message of encouragement, or even just sharing content that brings a smile to people's faces.

One powerful example of digital kindness is the concept of "Twitter kindness threads," where people share positive affirmations, encouraging messages, or even resources for those in need. These threads often go viral, not because they're controversial or shocking, but because they tap into a deep human need for connection and positivity. People retweet them, add their own kind words, and suddenly, what started as a simple thread becomes a movement, a reminder that kindness can spread even through the pixels of a screen.

The Lasting Imprint of a Single Kind Act

Kindness also has a way of staying with us, long after the moment has passed. It's like a tattoo on the heart—something that leaves a lasting mark, even if it was just a fleeting encounter. Think back to your childhood, to that teacher who encouraged you, or a neighbor who always welcomed you with a warm smile. Those moments stay with us, shaping our understanding of the world and our place in it. They become part of the stories we tell ourselves about who we are and what we believe people are capable of.

Take, for instance, the story of a man who, while walking through a park, noticed a little girl struggling to learn how to ride her bike. Her father was trying to help, but she was frustrated and on the verge of giving up. The man, a complete stranger, stopped, smiled at the girl, and said, "You've got this. Just one more try, and you'll get it." He stayed for a few minutes, offering encouragement, and then continued on his walk. To him, it was a small moment, something he probably forgot about soon after. But for that little girl, it was the difference between giving up and pushing through. Years later, she remembered that stranger's words every time she faced a new challenge.

This is the beauty of kindness—it's a legacy that extends beyond the moment, beyond even our own understanding. You may never know the full impact of your kind words, your actions, or your compassion, but that doesn't make them any less important. Like seeds carried by the wind, they may take root in places you'll never see, growing into something beautiful.

And what if we began to view our lives through this lens, seeing each interaction as an opportunity to plant seeds of kindness? What if we approached every day with the mindset that our words and actions have the potential to change someone's life? It's a mindset that doesn't just transform the people around us—it transforms us too. It makes us more mindful, more empathetic, more connected to the world and the people in it.

In this way, kindness becomes a practice, a daily intention to be a positive force, even in the smallest ways. It's about choosing to smile instead of frown, to listen instead of interrupt, to reach out instead of holding back. And as we make these choices, as we choose to be kind, we start to notice the ripples—both in the world around us and in ourselves. We start to see that being kind isn't just something we do—it's who we are.

Embracing Kindness in a World That Often Feels Unkind

But let's not pretend that choosing kindness is always easy. There are days when the world feels heavy, when it seems like kindness is in short supply, when people are rude, and the news is filled with stories that make you question humanity. On those days, kindness can feel like an uphill battle—a struggle against the tide of negativity. And yet, it's on those days that kindness is most needed.

Imagine a world where, even on the hardest days, people chose to be a little kinder. Where a driver stuck in traffic takes a deep breath and lets someone merge ahead of them, where a person in a hurry chooses to slow down and hold the elevator for someone else, where we all collectively decide that it's better to add a little bit of light than to contribute to the darkness.

It's a simple vision, but it's a powerful one. And the beauty of it is that we don't need to wait for anyone else to start—we can begin right now, with our next interaction, our next conversation, our next opportunity to make someone's day just a little bit brighter. Because, at the end of the day, kindness costs nothing, yet it's truly priceless.

And this is just the beginning of our exploration into the power of a kind gesture, the ripple effects that reach farther than we can imagine, and the ways in which a simple act can transform a life. As we move forward, we'll continue to see that the greatest changes often begin with the smallest acts—those that come from a place of genuine compassion, without any expectation of return.

As we reach the end of this chapter, let's take a moment to reflect on the simple yet profound truth that lies at the heart of kindness: its power to create a ripple effect that can transform lives. A kind gesture, no matter how small, holds the potential to set off a chain reaction—one that extends far beyond the initial act. The warmth you give to one person has the power to spread, touching lives in ways you may never see or know.

Every time we choose kindness, we plant a seed. Sometimes, it takes root quickly, like a smile that brightens someone's difficult day. Other times, it might remain hidden beneath the surface, only to bloom much later—perhaps at a moment when someone needs it most. But every seed matters. Every single one contributes to a world that is just a little more compassionate, a little more human.

In a society that often glorifies grand gestures and big achievements, it's easy to forget the power of the small things—holding a door, offering a listening ear, or sharing a word of encouragement. Yet, these moments are what stitch the fabric of our shared humanity. They remind us that, despite our differences, we are all connected by the same basic need for kindness, understanding, and connection.

And as we go forward in this book, we'll explore even more ways in which kindness shapes our relationships, our communities, and even our sense of self. We'll see how the simple decision to be kind can open doors to new possibilities and lead to a deeper sense of fulfillment. But before we move on, remember this: every time you choose to be kind, you are not just making a difference in someone else's life—you are making a difference in your own.

Because, in the end, kindness truly costs nothing. Yet, for those who receive it, and even more so for those who give it, it is absolutely priceless. The ripple you start today might be the one that changes the world for someone tomorrow. And in that quiet, unassuming way, kindness continues its journey—one heart at a time, one moment at a time, ever expanding its reach.

So, let's make the choice to be kind, knowing that the ripples we create can travel farther than we'll ever see, leaving behind a legacy of compassion, connection, and hope.

CHAPTER TWO

Kindness as a Superpower

There's a hidden strength that lives within us all, a force that doesn't rely on physical power or sharp intellect. It's subtle but immense, gentle yet capable of bringing about profound change. This strength is kindness—an unassuming superpower that has the potential to transform not only our own lives but the world around us. In a world that often equates power with dominance, kindness stands out as a quiet force, reshaping the way we connect, heal, and grow.

Why Empathy is a Strength, Not a Weakness

In a society where being tough and resilient is often celebrated, empathy—one of the core components of kindness—is sometimes seen as a vulnerability. The common belief is that those who feel deeply, who take time to understand the struggles of others, may be too sensitive or soft-hearted. But what if, instead, empathy is our greatest strength?

Imagine being able to step into someone else's shoes, to understand their feelings and see the world through their eyes. Empathy allows us to connect at a level beyond words. It means recognizing the invisible burdens that others carry, feeling their joys, and sharing in their struggles. Far from being a weakness, this ability to understand others can break down barriers and build bridges between hearts.

Empathy allows us to create genuine relationships, ones where people feel seen and valued. When a friend is struggling, it's empathy that helps us say, "I'm here for you," in a way that truly matters. It's the force that allows us to recognize when someone's bravado is masking pain or when silence is a cry for help.

And when kindness is powered by empathy, it becomes unstoppable. It's what makes us reach out when we see someone sitting alone, what drives us to lend a helping hand without expecting anything in return. It's what compels us to be patient with a coworker who's having a bad day or to listen deeply to a loved one's worries, even when our own plate is full.

Empathy, in this light, is not just about feeling for others—it's about acting on that feeling. It's about taking what you understand and turning it into action, using your insight to uplift, support, and bring comfort. That's why empathy, far from being a sign of fragility, is a cornerstone of true strength. It takes courage to open your heart to others, to risk feeling their pain along with them, but in doing so, you create connections that are real and enduring.

From Bullied to Beloved: How Kindness Changes Narratives

We often hear stories of people who have faced incredible adversity—those who have been mocked, marginalized, or made to feel small. Yet, among these stories, there are those who, through the simple yet powerful choice of kindness, turned their narratives around, shifting from being bullied to becoming beacons of hope for others.

Take, for example, the story of a young boy who was once an outcast, picked on for being different. He could have let the world's cruelty harden him, turning inward with bitterness. But instead, he chose kindness. He chose to smile at those who had hurt him, to befriend those who sat alone, and to offer help when others least expected it. Over time, those who once saw him as weak began to see him differently. His kindness softened their edges, and in turn, he became a source of inspiration—a reminder that there is strength in turning the other cheek.

Or consider the woman who, after years of being misunderstood, started a community group that focused on inclusion and acceptance. She channeled her own experiences of exclusion into creating a space where others could feel safe, welcomed, and valued. Her kindness transformed not just her own life but the lives of many who found in her a sense of belonging they had never known.

These stories aren't just about individuals—they're about the transformative power of kindness itself. When faced with negativity, kindness has the power to change the script. It allows us to redefine who we are, to shift from being victims of circumstance to agents of change. And in doing so, we discover a superpower that can alter not just our own lives but the entire story for those around us.

Turning Challenges into Opportunities for Kindness

Life is full of challenges, from the mundane frustrations of daily life to the deep sorrows that shake us to our core. It's easy to react with frustration, to allow anger or bitterness to seep in when things don't go our way. But what if we saw every challenge as an opportunity for kindness—a chance to show grace under pressure, to be a light in dark times?

Imagine standing in a long line at the grocery store, feeling the impatience building up inside you. You notice the cashier struggling, the stress visible on their face. Instead of letting the annoyance win, you take a breath and offer a kind word, a simple "You're doing great, hang in there." It's a small act, but it can make a world of difference.

Or think about those moments when life throws something truly difficult your way—like a job loss or the end of a relationship. It's easy to become consumed by our own pain during such times. But in choosing to extend kindness outward, even when we're hurting, we often find that our own burdens become a little lighter. By volunteering, helping a neighbor, or simply reaching out to a friend in need, we transform our struggles into acts of love.

This isn't about pretending everything is okay or ignoring our own needs. It's about recognizing that in the toughest moments, kindness has a way of expanding our hearts, giving us the strength to endure.

It's about finding the courage to be compassionate, even when it would be easier to retreat into our own hurt. And in doing so, we discover a resilience that carries us through.

Kindness, when wielded during difficult times, is like a lantern in the darkness. It illuminates not only the path for others but for ourselves. It gives us purpose when life feels aimless and brings hope when everything seems bleak. And as we continue on this journey of exploring the power of kindness, we'll see just how much these small, intentional choices can shift the course of our lives—and those of everyone we touch.

As we dig deeper into the nature of kindness, it becomes clear that this unassuming power is about much more than just being "nice." It's about a conscious choice to uplift others, even when it's inconvenient, uncomfortable, or against the grain. True kindness doesn't look for recognition or applause—it's driven by an inner compass that recognizes the humanity in others and responds to it, no matter the circumstances.

Empathy in Action: Changing the Conversation

Empathy is not a passive feeling; it's an active engagement with the world around us. To understand someone else's pain or joy is the first step, but to act on that understanding is what makes empathy a strength. In a world that often rushes past moments of connection, taking the time to slow down and truly see another person is a radical act. It's a form of rebellion against a society that teaches us to prioritize self-interest above all else.

Picture a busy subway station during rush hour. Most people are absorbed in their own lives—heads down, scrolling through phones, or hurrying to their next destination. But in the corner, there's an older man struggling with a heavy bag. Amidst the crowd, one person notices, steps forward, and offers help. It's a small moment, a mere blip in the day's chaos, yet it has the power to shift the atmosphere. This act of empathy becomes a story shared over dinner, a reminder that amidst the anonymity of the city, there is still space for kindness.

Empathy like this has a ripple effect. It can transform a place, turning a cold, impersonal environment into one where people remember that they are not alone. This is the superpower that kindness holds—one that creates a space for others to feel seen, heard, and valued. And while the individual act may seem small, its impact is anything but.

The Courage to Be Kind When It's Hard

Kindness is easy when life is good, when the sun is shining and everything is going according to plan. But its true power reveals itself in difficult times—when patience wears thin, when hurt or anger might feel justified, and when showing kindness seems like a challenge rather than a natural response.

Consider the story of a young woman named Sarah, who faced relentless criticism at her workplace. She could have easily become defensive, retaliating with sharp words. Instead, Sarah chose a different path. She began to listen deeply to her critics, acknowledging their frustrations without letting their negativity consume her. She offered kindness even when it wasn't deserved, creating an atmosphere of mutual respect.

At first, her colleagues didn't know what to make of her approach. But over time, her refusal to respond with anger began to shift the dynamic. People softened around her, conversations became more constructive, and the office tension eased. By choosing kindness in the face of criticism, Sarah wasn't just making her life easier—she was leading by example, showing that kindness could be a powerful tool for change.

Sarah's story illustrates an important truth: kindness requires courage. It asks us to be vulnerable, to let go of our need for validation, and to give without expecting anything in return. This is what makes it so powerful. In a world where so many interactions are transactional, being kind for the sake of kindness itself stands out—it disrupts the norm and challenges others to rise to a higher standard.

Kindness in Leadership: The Strength to Lift Others Up

We often think of leaders as people who wield authority, who command attention and guide others through strength and vision. But some of the most impactful leaders are those who lead with kindness, who use their influence to uplift rather than dominate. These leaders understand that kindness is not about being "soft"; it's about recognizing the potential in others and helping them grow.

Think about the mentors who shaped your life. Chances are, they weren't the ones who simply told you what to do or pointed out your flaws. They were the ones who believed in you when you doubted yourself, who took the time to listen to your fears, and who guided you with patience. Their kindness gave you the space to fail, to learn, and to eventually succeed.

Leadership through kindness means being willing to give others the credit, to acknowledge their contributions, and to create an environment where people feel safe to express themselves. It's about understanding that every person, no matter their role, brings value to the table. And when people feel valued, they thrive. They bring their best selves to their work, to their relationships, and to the world.

This kind of leadership isn't always easy. It requires a deep sense of empathy, a willingness to put others' needs before your own, and the patience to nurture growth even when progress is slow. But the impact it has—on individuals, on teams, and on entire communities—can be profound.

Turning Pain into Purpose Through Kindness

One of the most transformative aspects of kindness is its ability to turn our own pain into purpose. When we experience hardship, it's natural to feel isolated, to believe that our struggles separate us from others. But kindness offers a way out of that isolation. It gives us a chance to use our pain as a bridge, connecting with others who might be going through something similar.

There's a powerful story of a man named John, who lost a loved one in a tragic accident. For a long time, he felt consumed by grief, unsure of how to move forward. But one day, he decided to volunteer at a support group for others who had experienced loss. He began to share his story, offering comfort to those who were in the early stages of their grief.

John's kindness didn't erase his pain—it didn't bring back what he had lost. But it gave his suffering a new meaning. By being there for others, he found a sense of purpose that helped him heal. He discovered that his own experiences of loss had made him uniquely capable of offering empathy and understanding to those who needed it most. And in helping others find their way through the darkness, he found his own path back to light.

This is the paradox of kindness: it's in giving to others that we often find the strength we need for ourselves. It's in offering a shoulder to cry on that we feel our own burdens lighten, in being there for someone else that we realize we are not alone. Kindness doesn't erase the challenges we face, but it gives us a way to transform them, to turn our wounds into sources of strength.

Empathy: The True Measure of Human Strength

Empathy is often misunderstood as a form of emotional fragility, a softness that doesn't belong in a world obsessed with success, competition, and individual achievement. But in reality, empathy is a profound source of strength—one that helps us navigate the complexities of life with grace and a deep sense of humanity. It allows us to understand emotions beyond words, to see through the facades people often wear, and to connect with the raw, unfiltered reality of their experiences.

Let's imagine a high-stakes corporate environment, a world where pressure to meet targets and deadlines dominates every interaction. Amidst the constant rush, there is a manager, Ravi, who makes a point to ask his team members how they're doing—not just as a formality, but with genuine interest. When one of his team members, Alicia, starts missing deadlines and showing signs of stress, Ravi doesn't reprimand her immediately. Instead, he takes her aside and asks, "Is everything okay?"

At first, Alicia hesitates—she's not used to being asked about her feelings at work. But seeing the sincerity in Ravi's eyes, she opens up about her struggles at home, the health issues her family is facing, and how it's impacting her focus. Ravi listens without interrupting, without offering immediate solutions, just being present for her. After their conversation, he helps her adjust her workload temporarily, connects her with resources, and checks in regularly to ensure she's doing better.

In that moment, Ravi's empathy wasn't just an act of kindness—it was an act of leadership, creating a space where Alicia felt valued as a human being, not just as an employee. That small gesture not only helped Alicia through a difficult time but also built a bond of trust between them that transformed their working relationship. Alicia's productivity improved as her personal situation stabilized, and she remained fiercely loyal to the team, knowing that her well-being truly mattered to Ravi.

Empathy like this isn't just a personal trait—it's a skill that can be cultivated, practiced, and refined. It's about learning to listen without judgment, to put yourself in someone else's shoes even when their experiences are vastly different from your own. It's about recognizing that every person you meet is carrying a burden you might not see, and choosing to be a little gentler with them because of it. And in this way, empathy becomes a superpower, one that transforms relationships, fosters resilience, and builds a sense of community in even the most unlikely places.

From Victim to Victor: The Transformative Power of Kindness

Kindness has the power to rewrite narratives, especially for those who have experienced bullying, rejection, or feelings of inadequacy. Many of us carry scars from times when we were made to feel less than, when unkind words or actions left a lasting impact on our self-worth. But kindness can be the healing balm for those wounds, a force that helps us reclaim our power and transform from victims into victors.

Take the story of Daniel, a teenager who spent most of his school years being bullied for his quiet demeanor and unique interests. His classmates taunted him for being different, turning his days into a series of small humiliations. Daniel withdrew into himself, feeling like he would never be accepted for who he was. His self-confidence withered, and he began to believe the hurtful things others said about him.

But everything changed when he met Mrs. Patel, a teacher who took a special interest in him. She saw potential in Daniel that others overlooked—his creative mind, his passion for storytelling, his empathy towards others. Instead of dismissing him as shy or awkward, she encouraged him to share his thoughts in class, praised his writing, and paired him with students who appreciated his unique perspective.

Mrs. Patel's kindness was the turning point for Daniel. It didn't just change the way others saw him; it changed the way he saw himself. Her belief in him gave him the courage to stand up to the bullies, to reclaim his voice, and to eventually find friends who valued him for who he was. Years later, when Daniel graduated as valedictorian, he credited her in his speech, saying, "Your kindness was the light in my darkest days. You made me believe that I mattered, that I was more than what others said about me."

Daniel's story is a testament to the transformative power of kindness. It shows how a single act of belief, a single voice of encouragement, can change the entire trajectory of a person's life. Kindness, in this way, becomes a superpower that allows us to rewrite our own stories and to help others do the same. It reminds us that we are not defined by the cruelty we've faced but by the strength we find within ourselves to rise above it.

Challenges as Catalysts for Kindness

Life is full of challenges, and many of them can feel like walls that stand between us and our happiness. Yet, if we shift our perspective, these very challenges can become opportunities to show kindness—to ourselves and to others. They become moments where we can choose to respond with compassion instead of resentment, with understanding instead of frustration.

Think of a time when you faced a difficult situation—a job loss, a breakup, or a serious health scare. It's easy to become bitter in those moments, to retreat into a shell and see the world through a lens of pain. But imagine if, in the midst of that difficulty, you found a way to extend kindness to someone else—a stranger, a friend, or even yourself.

This is what happened to Maya when she lost her job during a tough economic downturn. At first, the news left her devastated; she felt like the ground had been pulled out from under her feet. But instead of letting despair consume her, Maya decided to use her newfound time to volunteer at a local food bank. She figured that helping others might help her find a sense of purpose amidst the uncertainty.

At the food bank, she met families who were struggling far more than she was—parents who couldn't afford groceries, elderly folks who lived alone, teenagers who had to balance school with part-time jobs to support their siblings. Maya listened to their stories, offered them a warm smile and a few words of encouragement, and made sure they left with enough food to last them through the week.

In those moments, Maya found a new perspective on her own situation. She realized that while she had lost a job, she hadn't lost her ability to give. She hadn't lost her compassion or her capacity to make a difference. Volunteering didn't magically solve all her problems, but it helped her feel connected to others, gave her a sense of purpose, and reminded her that even in tough times, there is always room for kindness.

Eventually, Maya found a new job—one that aligned better with her values and passions. But she continued to volunteer at the food bank on weekends, not because she needed to, but because she wanted to. The experience had changed her, deepening her empathy and making her more attuned to the struggles of those around her.

Maya's story teaches us that challenges don't have to harden us. They can become the soil in which the seeds of kindness grow, turning adversity into an opportunity for connection and growth. When we choose to respond to our struggles with compassion, we not only uplift others but also find a sense of strength and purpose within ourselves.

Kindness: The Bridge to Connection

One of the most powerful aspects of kindness is its ability to build connections—sometimes with people you've known for years, other times with complete strangers whose lives brush against yours for just a fleeting moment. This kind of connection, born out of simple gestures and genuine compassion, creates a sense of belonging that's often hard to find in our fast-paced, digital world. It's a reminder that no matter how different our backgrounds, beliefs, or circumstances might be, there is a fundamental human thread that binds us all.

Consider the story of Carlos, a commuter who took the same train every day to his job downtown. One chilly winter morning, he noticed an elderly man struggling to carry his groceries up the stairs at the train station. Most people walked past, too focused on their own routines to pay much attention. But Carlos decided to stop and lend a hand, even though he knew it meant he might miss his train.

The elderly man, Mr. Lee, was initially hesitant. He wasn't used to receiving help, preferring to maintain his independence even as his physical strength waned. But Carlos insisted, carrying the heavy bags up the stairs and chatting with Mr. Lee as they walked. They found out that they lived just a few blocks away from each other, and over the next few weeks, their small morning conversations turned into something of a routine.

As they shared stories of their lives—Carlos about his young daughter and his love for playing guitar, Mr. Lee about his late wife and his time as a carpenter—they realized that these conversations were something they both looked forward to. Carlos wasn't just helping Mr. Lee with his groceries anymore; he was building a relationship that brought warmth and meaning to both of their mornings. For Carlos, it was a reminder of the wisdom and stories held within the older generations, and for Mr. Lee, it was a chance to feel seen and valued again.

Their connection wasn't extraordinary in the sense that it made headlines or went viral on social media. It didn't change the world in a grand way. But it changed their worlds, brightening their days and adding a sense of community to what might have otherwise been lonely moments. And in the end, isn't that what kindness is truly about? It's not always about grand gestures or monumental acts—it's about the small, steady bridge that kindness builds between hearts.

This bridge has the power to extend far beyond our everyday circles. When we show kindness to strangers, it can create an invisible web of goodwill that we might never fully see, but whose effects can ripple through countless lives. Imagine the impact of smiling at a stressed cashier, of letting a car merge in front of you during rush hour, of leaving an extra tip for a hardworking server. Each small act may seem insignificant on its own, but collectively, they create a world where people feel more appreciated, where empathy flows more freely, and where connections form in places where there was once only indifference.

Empathy in Action: Walking in Someone Else's Shoes

Empathy doesn't just change how we perceive others; it also transforms our own actions, inspiring us to go beyond what is expected or convenient. When we take a moment to imagine what someone else might be going through, our perspective shifts, and so do our priorities. This shift is often the starting point for acts of kindness that truly make a difference.

Let's revisit Ravi's story—remember, the manager who showed empathy to his struggling employee, Alicia? After helping Alicia through her personal struggles, Ravi found himself reflecting on the nature of empathy itself. He realized that empathy wasn't just about being a good listener; it was about understanding the unspoken, about sensing the pain that people might carry without ever saying a word.

This realization led him to initiate a new policy at his office: a monthly "Empathy Circle," where team members could gather in a judgment-free space to share their experiences and challenges. It wasn't mandatory, but those who chose to attend quickly found that it became a highlight of their month. In these circles, people shared stories of juggling parenthood with work, of grieving losses, of battling mental health challenges that they had kept hidden out of fear of judgment.

These circles transformed the office culture, turning it into a place where people felt more seen and supported than ever before. Productivity soared, not because of stricter deadlines or more demanding targets, but because people felt they could bring their whole selves to work. They trusted each other, and that trust led to more collaborative projects, innovative ideas, and a sense of loyalty that was unshakeable.

For Ravi, it was a powerful reminder that empathy in action doesn't just help individuals—it can reshape entire communities. It's not always easy to carve out time for kindness in a busy world, but when we make the effort, the results can be profound. People become more than their roles, more than their labels, and in that shared humanity, we find a strength that propels us forward.

Kindness During Crisis: A Lifeline in Dark Times

While kindness is often a choice we make in our daily lives, it becomes a lifeline when we face crises—those moments when life throws challenges at us that seem too big to handle alone. In times of disaster, loss, or uncertainty, kindness reveals itself as a powerful force that helps us survive, rebuild, and ultimately heal.

Think about the aftermath of natural disasters like hurricanes, wildfires, or floods. These events often leave behind a trail of destruction, displacing families, destroying homes, and turning lives upside down in a matter of hours. But amidst the devastation, there are always stories of strangers helping strangers—people opening their doors to those in need, communities coming together to organize relief efforts, volunteers traveling hundreds of miles just to lend a hand.

One such story comes from the aftermath of a devastating flood in a small town in the Midwest. The floodwaters had risen quickly, catching many residents off guard and forcing them to evacuate with little more than the clothes on their backs. In the days that followed, the town's community center became a makeshift shelter, providing food, blankets, and a warm place to sleep for those who had lost everything.

Among the volunteers was a teenager named Elena, who had just graduated high school and was planning to leave for college. She could have spent her summer celebrating with friends or preparing for her new life in the city, but instead, she chose to stay behind and help with the relief efforts. She spent hours sorting through donations, serving meals, and comforting children who were struggling to make sense of the chaos around them.

During one particularly busy night, Elena met an elderly couple who had lost their home to the flood. They were disoriented, their eyes filled with a mixture of fear and exhaustion. Elena sat with them, listening to their stories about the house they had lived in for over fifty years, about the memories that had been washed away. She didn't have the power to bring back what they had lost, but she offered them a kind ear, a cup of hot tea, and a promise that they wouldn't have to face this alone.

The next morning, the couple gave Elena a small, water-damaged photo of their family, the only possession they had managed to save. "Thank you for being here," they said. "We didn't know anyone would care enough to listen." Elena kept that photo as a reminder that kindness isn't about fixing everything; it's about being there when it matters most, about offering what you can, even if it's just a few moments of your time.

In the end, the town began to rebuild, homes were repaired, and life slowly returned to normal. But the memory of those days in the shelter stayed with Elena, shaping her outlook on life and her sense of purpose. She realized that even when everything else is stripped away, kindness remains—a small light that guides us through the darkest times.

Kindness: The True Superpower Within

As we bring this chapter to a close, it's clear that kindness isn't just a fleeting act or a gentle word; it's a superpower that resides within each of us, ready to shape the world in ways big and small. While it doesn't grant the ability to fly or move mountains, kindness can uplift a heavy heart, bridge divides, and create waves of change that extend far beyond the moment.

Empathy, often mistaken for a weakness, reveals its strength when we dare to truly see others—to listen to their stories and feel their struggles. It allows us to turn simple interactions into lasting connections, and it transforms challenges into opportunities for growth and understanding. Empathy is the fuel that powers kindness, pushing us to step outside of our own perspectives and make a difference, no matter how small.

Kindness also thrives in the unlikeliest of places, revealing its power when we face adversity. It is in these moments of crisis that the essence of humanity shines through—when a community bands together after a disaster, when strangers extend a helping hand, or when a few comforting words become a lifeline for someone struggling to hold on. These acts, no matter how small they may seem, are the threads that weave a stronger, more compassionate world.

But perhaps the greatest lesson of all is that kindness doesn't require extraordinary circumstances; it flourishes in the everyday. It's the smile you give a stranger, the understanding you extend to a colleague, the time you take to listen without judgment. It's the courage to show compassion even when it's inconvenient, and the grace to choose empathy over indifference.

And as we reflect on the stories and lessons shared in this chapter, let's remember that kindness is not something we give expecting something in return. It is a way of life, a mindset that says, "I see you,

I care, and I'm here to make things a little better." It's a gift that costs nothing, yet it holds the potential to be priceless in someone else's life.

In the end, kindness is a superpower because it has the ability to change us as much as it changes those around us. It transforms our hearts, deepens our connections, and reminds us of the simple truth that we are all in this together. So, let's embrace the power of kindness, not as a rare act, but as a daily choice—a choice to make the world a bit warmer, a bit kinder, and a bit more connected, one small gesture at a time.

CHAPTER THREE

The Science Behind Kindness

The idea that kindness is good for the soul is ancient wisdom, often passed down through generations. But as science advances, we're learning that this old saying holds more truth than we ever realized. Behind every act of kindness lies a series of fascinating biological and psychological processes that are reshaping our understanding of how kindness impacts not just the world around us, but our own bodies and minds.

How Acts of Kindness Boost Mental Health

Imagine a day where you go out of your way to help someone—a neighbor struggling with their groceries, a colleague facing a tight deadline, or even a stranger who seems a little down. These seemingly small actions don't just leave the recipient feeling grateful; they actually trigger a powerful reaction within us too. When we engage in kind acts, our brains release a cocktail of chemicals—endorphins, dopamine, and serotonin. It's what researchers like to call "the helper's high."

The Helper's High: A Natural Antidepressant

Science has shown that when we perform acts of kindness, we experience a natural rush of feel-good chemicals, similar to what athletes experience during a runner's high. This surge helps to reduce stress levels and boost our mood. Studies have found that even witnessing acts of kindness can trigger this effect. For example, seeing someone help an elderly person cross the street or offering support to someone in need can lead to an immediate uplift in mood. This is due to the activation of certain brain regions associated with pleasure and reward, such as the ventral striatum.

But the benefits don't stop at a temporary mood boost. Regularly engaging in kind acts has been linked to long-term improvements in mental health. Psychologists have found that individuals who make kindness a habit are less likely to suffer from anxiety and depression. By focusing on the well-being of others, we often shift our perspective away from our own worries and stresses, giving our minds a much-needed break from negative thought patterns.

Kindness as a Stress Buster

In a world where stress has become a constant companion for many of us, kindness offers a powerful antidote. Engaging in compassionate actions has been shown to lower levels of cortisol, the stress hormone that can wreak havoc on our bodies when it remains elevated for too long. In one study, participants who engaged in a daily act of kindness for just one month reported significant decreases in stress levels, feeling calmer and more at ease with themselves and their surroundings.

This isn't just about grand gestures—small acts like offering a compliment or writing a note of appreciation can have a profound effect. As the stress begins to melt away, it's replaced by a sense of purpose and connection that has a lasting impact on our overall mental well-being.

The Social Connection Factor

Kindness also strengthens our sense of social connection, which is crucial for mental health. Human beings are inherently social creatures, and feeling connected to others can reduce feelings of loneliness and isolation, which are often at the root of many mental health challenges. When we show kindness, we often receive kindness in return, creating a positive feedback loop that deepens our social bonds and enhances our sense of belonging.

In fact, research has shown that people who engage in altruistic behaviors tend to have better relationships and a stronger support network. And when we feel supported by those around us, we're better equipped to handle life's challenges. Whether it's a small gesture like holding the door open for someone or a larger act like volunteering, every bit of kindness helps build a more connected and resilient community.

The Biology of a Kind Heart: How Our Brain Reacts to Kindness

Underneath the warm and fuzzy feelings we get from being kind lies a complex web of biological processes. The brain is a remarkable organ that processes kindness in unique ways, affecting everything from our hormones to our neural pathways.

Oxytocin: The Love Hormone and Kindness

One of the key players in this process is oxytocin, often referred to as the "love hormone." Oxytocin is released when we engage in acts of kindness, whether it's a simple hug or offering a listening ear. This hormone is known for its role in promoting feelings of trust, bonding, and empathy. It's why a kind gesture can make us feel closer to someone, even if we've just met them.

Oxytocin also has physical benefits—it helps lower blood pressure, reduce inflammation, and even accelerate the healing of wounds. This is one reason why kind individuals often report feeling healthier and more energized. The release of oxytocin creates a sense of warmth and connection that enhances our overall well-being.

Dopamine: The Reward System at Play

Another crucial player is dopamine, the neurotransmitter associated with pleasure and reward. When we do something kind, the brain's reward center lights up, releasing dopamine and giving us a natural "high." This is why kindness can be so addictive; the more we engage in it, the more we want to keep doing it.

Interestingly, this dopamine rush doesn't just occur when we actively perform acts of kindness—it also happens when we reflect on past kind actions. This means that even thinking about times when you were kind can provide a boost to your mood and mental state. It's like a built-in reward system that keeps reinforcing positive behavior, making kindness not only beneficial but also deeply satisfying.

Mirror Neurons: Feeling What Others Feel

Our brains are also equipped with mirror neurons, which fire both when we perform an action and when we observe someone else performing the same action. This is what allows us to feel empathy—to sense the joy or pain of others as if it were our own. When we see someone being kind, our mirror neurons respond, making us feel the warmth and positivity of that action. It's why witnessing kindness can be just as powerful as experiencing it directly.

This neurological response doesn't just promote empathy; it also motivates us to act. When we see someone being kind, we're more likely to want to perform a kind act ourselves. It's as if our brains are wired to spread kindness, creating a ripple effect that can transform entire communities.

Kindness and Longevity: The Secret to a Happy Life

As we delve deeper into the science behind kindness, one of the most surprising discoveries is its impact on longevity. While diet, exercise, and genetics all play a role in determining how long we live, kindness seems to be a powerful yet often overlooked factor in promoting a longer, healthier life.

The Longevity Studies: Kindness Extends Life

Numerous studies have found a correlation between kindness and longevity. For example, research has shown that individuals who volunteer regularly tend to live longer than those who don't. The reason? Volunteering often involves social interaction, physical activity, and a sense of purpose—all of which contribute to better physical and mental health. It's as if the act of giving our time and energy to others adds time to our own lives.

One groundbreaking study followed elderly individuals who regularly provided support to friends, family, or their community. Those who were consistently kind and involved in altruistic activities were more likely to live longer than those who were less engaged. It turns out that the positive effects of kindness don't just stop at the mind—they extend to the heart and body as well.

Stress Reduction and Cardiovascular Health

Stress is a major factor in many chronic illnesses, from heart disease to diabetes. By reducing stress levels, kindness indirectly promotes better cardiovascular health. Lower cortisol levels mean a lower risk of high blood pressure, heart attacks, and strokes. It's like a natural shield against the wear and tear that stress can have on our bodies over time.

The connection between kindness and a healthier heart is so strong that some scientists have even suggested prescribing kindness as part of a treatment plan for heart patients. When we practice kindness, we're not just improving our mood—we're taking a proactive step toward a longer, healthier life.

A Sense of Purpose: The Ultimate Life Extender

Kindness also gives us a sense of purpose, which has been shown to be one of the most important factors in living a long and fulfilling life. When we know that our actions matter, that we have the power to make a difference in someone else's life, it provides a deep sense of meaning. This sense of purpose acts as a buffer against the existential struggles that many people face, especially as they age.

In societies known for their longevity, such as the Okinawans in Japan, a sense of community and mutual support is deeply ingrained in their way of life. People look out for one another, offering help and kindness as a natural part of their daily routine. This culture of kindness is one of the reasons why these communities have a higher percentage of centenarians—people living to 100 years or more—than anywhere else in the world.

Kindness, it seems, is not just about making life better for others; it's a powerful way to enhance our own lives as well. Whether through the release of feel-good chemicals, the strengthening of social connections, or the deep sense of purpose it provides, kindness has the power to transform us from the inside out.

Kindness and Its Influence on Our Immune System

As we continue to unravel the layers of kindness, we uncover its profound impact on our physical health, particularly our immune system. The connection between our mental state and physical health has been a topic of extensive research, and kindness plays a crucial role in this relationship.

Boosting Immunity Through Kindness

Engaging in acts of kindness can significantly enhance our immune response. Studies have shown that individuals who practice kindness regularly tend to have higher levels of antibodies and immune cells. This means that by simply being kind, we're not only improving our mental state but also fortifying our bodies against illness.

For example, one study measured the immune responses of participants who volunteered in community service. Researchers found that those who engaged in acts of kindness displayed increased levels of immunoglobulin A (IgA), an antibody that plays a crucial role in the immune function. The results suggested that kindness could potentially offer a protective effect against various infections and diseases.

The Role of Positive Emotions

The mechanism behind this immune boost is rooted in the emotions associated with kindness. When we act kindly, we experience positive emotions that trigger the release of hormones like oxytocin and endorphins, which have been linked to improved immune function. These hormones not only help alleviate stress but also promote overall health, creating a virtuous cycle where kindness begets health, and good health inspires further acts of kindness.

Social Connectivity and Immune Function

The social connections forged through kindness are also vital for our immune health. Strong social ties have been shown to correlate with better immune function, while social isolation can lead to adverse health outcomes. By being part of a community that values kindness, we inherently enhance our immune systems and overall well-being.

The importance of community in fostering a culture of kindness cannot be understated. When we surround ourselves with individuals who prioritize kindness, we create an environment where support and compassion flourish. This support network serves as a buffer against stress and its negative health effects, ultimately leading to improved immune function.

Kindness and Mental Resilience

Beyond its physical health benefits, kindness plays a pivotal role in developing mental resilience. Life is rife with challenges, from personal setbacks to global crises, and the ability to bounce back from adversity is crucial for maintaining mental health. Engaging in kind acts not only helps us cope with our struggles but also fortifies our ability to face future challenges.

Building Mental Fortitude Through Kindness

Research has shown that people who regularly practice kindness tend to have greater mental resilience. This resilience is linked to the positive emotional experiences that come from helping others. When we engage in acts of kindness, we experience a sense of accomplishment and self-worth, which can help us navigate life's challenges more effectively.

Consider the example of individuals who volunteer in crisis situations. Those who provide support during natural disasters or humanitarian crises often report a profound sense of purpose and fulfillment. This engagement not only helps those in need but also builds a sense of mental fortitude within the volunteers themselves, equipping them with the emotional strength to handle their own life challenges.

Kindness as a Coping Mechanism

Furthermore, kindness serves as a powerful coping mechanism during difficult times. When we face personal struggles—be it a loss, a health scare, or financial difficulties—turning our focus outward and helping others can alleviate our own pain. Acts of kindness distract us from our troubles and remind us of the goodness still present in the world. This shift in focus can foster a sense of gratitude, which is closely linked to improved mental health.

Studies indicate that gratitude is a vital component of resilience. By practicing kindness and reflecting on the positive impact we have on others, we cultivate an attitude of gratitude that bolsters our mental health. This gratitude helps us reframe our challenges, allowing us to view them through a more optimistic lens.

Kindness in the Workplace: Boosting Morale and Productivity

The benefits of kindness extend beyond personal interactions and seep into our professional lives as well. In workplaces where kindness is prioritized, employees report higher levels of job satisfaction, better morale, and increased productivity.

Creating a Culture of Kindness

Organizations that foster a culture of kindness often see lower turnover rates and higher employee engagement. When employees feel supported and valued, they are more likely to go above and beyond in their roles. Simple acts of kindness—such as acknowledging a colleague's hard work, offering assistance on a project, or expressing gratitude—can significantly boost workplace morale.

Kindness as a Leadership Trait

Leadership plays a crucial role in establishing this culture. Leaders who demonstrate kindness set the tone for the entire organization. When leaders show empathy and understanding, it creates an environment where employees feel safe and valued. This, in turn, leads to a more collaborative and innovative workplace.

Research has shown that kindness in leadership can lead to increased productivity. Employees are more motivated to contribute to a positive work environment when they feel cared for by their leaders. This sense of loyalty often translates into higher levels of engagement and productivity.

The Positive Ripple Effect in Organizations

Furthermore, kindness can create a ripple effect within organizations. When one person performs a kind act, it inspires others to do the same, fostering a culture of generosity and support. This not only enhances relationships among colleagues but also improves overall team dynamics.

In one study conducted in various workplaces, researchers found that when employees engaged in acts of kindness, they reported feeling happier and more fulfilled in their roles. This happiness spread throughout the organization, leading to a collective boost in morale and job satisfaction.

Cultivating Kindness: Practical Steps to Incorporate in Daily Life

Understanding the benefits of kindness is just the first step; the real challenge lies in incorporating it into our daily lives. Here are some practical steps to cultivate kindness in everyday situations:

1. **Start Small**: Acts of kindness don't have to be grand. Start with small gestures, such as smiling at a stranger, complimenting a colleague, or holding the door open for

someone. These small acts can create a chain reaction, inspiring others to pay it forward.

2. **Practice Gratitude**: Take time each day to reflect on the things you're grateful for. Expressing gratitude not only boosts your mood but also encourages you to spread kindness to others.

3. **Volunteer Your Time**: Find opportunities to volunteer in your community. Whether it's helping at a local shelter, participating in a clean-up drive, or mentoring someone in need, volunteering provides an excellent avenue to engage in kindness.

4. **Listen Actively**: Sometimes, all someone needs is a listening ear. Practice active listening by giving your full attention to others when they speak. This simple act can create a profound impact on someone's day.

5. **Create Kindness Challenges**: Encourage friends, family, or colleagues to participate in kindness challenges. Set a goal to perform a certain number of kind acts within a week or month, and share your experiences with one another.

6. **Model Kindness for Others**: Be a role model for kindness, especially for younger generations. Demonstrate compassionate behavior, and encourage children and peers to engage in kind acts.

7. **Reflect on Kindness**: At the end of each day, take a moment to reflect on your acts of kindness. Consider how they made you feel and how they may have impacted others. This reflection can deepen your appreciation for kindness and motivate you to continue.

The Link Between Kindness and Stress Reduction

As we explore the intricacies of kindness, it becomes clear that one of its most significant impacts lies in its ability to reduce stress. In today's fast-paced world, where stress has become a pervasive issue affecting millions, the need for effective coping mechanisms has never been more crucial. Research shows that practicing kindness can significantly alleviate stress and its harmful effects on our health.

Understanding the Stress Response

The human body is equipped with a complex stress response system, often referred to as the fight-or-flight response. When faced with stress, our bodies release hormones such as adrenaline and cortisol, which prepare us to either confront the threat or flee from it. While this response is essential for survival, chronic activation due to ongoing stress can lead to serious health problems, including anxiety disorders, depression, and cardiovascular issues.

The Calming Effect of Kindness

Engaging in acts of kindness has been shown to counteract this stress response. When we help others, our brains release neurotransmitters like serotonin and oxytocin, commonly known as the "feel-good" hormones. These chemicals promote feelings of happiness and well-being, which can directly reduce the levels of stress hormones in our bodies.

A study conducted by researchers at the University of California, Berkeley, found that individuals who performed acts of kindness experienced lower levels of stress and anxiety. The participants reported feeling a sense of peace and contentment after engaging in acts of compassion, leading to a notable reduction in stress levels.

Kindness in the Face of Personal Struggles

In times of personal hardship, kindness can serve as a powerful antidote to stress. When we face challenges—whether they be health-related, financial, or emotional—turning our focus toward helping others can alleviate our burdens. This shift not only provides a distraction from our troubles but also instills a sense of purpose and fulfillment, which is particularly beneficial during difficult times.

Consider the story of a woman named Maria, who faced significant personal challenges after losing her job. Instead of succumbing to despair, she decided to volunteer at a local food bank. Through her efforts to help others, she discovered a newfound sense of strength and resilience. Not only did volunteering distract her from her own struggles, but it also allowed her to connect with others facing similar challenges. The kindness she extended to those in need ultimately transformed her own perspective and reduced her stress.

The Impact of Kindness on Relationships

In addition to its individual benefits, kindness profoundly influences our relationships. The connections we forge with others are vital to our emotional well-being, and kindness serves as a foundation for building strong, meaningful relationships.

Fostering Deeper Connections

Acts of kindness enhance our ability to connect with others on a deeper level. When we show kindness, we communicate empathy and understanding, which fosters trust and intimacy. These positive interactions can help bridge gaps between individuals, creating a sense of belonging that is essential for emotional health.

Research from the University of Pennsylvania has shown that relationships characterized by kindness and compassion are more resilient to conflicts. Couples who prioritize kindness in their interactions report higher levels of satisfaction and lower levels of conflict. This demonstrates that kindness not only strengthens bonds but also acts as a protective factor during challenging times.

The Role of Kindness in Conflict Resolution

In relationships, conflicts are inevitable. However, how we respond to these conflicts can either strengthen or weaken our connections. Kindness plays a critical role in conflict resolution, allowing us to approach disagreements with empathy and understanding.

When we practice kindness during conflicts, we create an environment that encourages open communication. Instead of resorting to blame or hostility, we can address issues with compassion, fostering constructive dialogue. This approach not only helps resolve conflicts more effectively but also reinforces the idea that our relationships are built on mutual respect and care.

Cultivating Kindness in Family Dynamics

In family relationships, kindness is particularly essential. Families often navigate various challenges, from parenting struggles to intergenerational conflicts. By prioritizing kindness within the family unit, we create an atmosphere of support and understanding.

For instance, parents who model kindness and compassion can instill these values in their children. This not only enhances family dynamics but also equips children with essential social skills that will benefit them in their relationships outside the home. When children observe their parents engaging in acts of kindness, they are more likely to emulate these behaviors in their interactions with peers and others.

The Cultural Perspective on Kindness

As we delve deeper into the science of kindness, it's essential to recognize that kindness is not only a personal trait but also a cultural one. Different cultures place varying degrees of emphasis on kindness and compassion, shaping how individuals express and receive kindness.

Cultural Variations in Kindness

In some cultures, kindness is woven into the fabric of daily life. For instance, in many collectivist societies, communal support and acts of kindness are fundamental values. People are encouraged to engage in helping behaviors, and these acts are often celebrated within the community.

In contrast, in more individualistic cultures, kindness may be less emphasized, leading individuals to prioritize personal success over communal well-being. This divergence can influence how people perceive and engage in acts of kindness, affecting the overall sense of community and social connectedness.

Global Movements Promoting Kindness

In recent years, there has been a growing recognition of the importance of kindness on a global scale. Initiatives such as World Kindness Day and the Kindness Rocks Project aim to promote acts of kindness and foster a culture of compassion worldwide. These movements encourage individuals to share their experiences of kindness and inspire others to do the same.

The Role of Technology in Spreading Kindness

Technology has also played a significant role in amplifying kindness across cultures. Social media platforms provide a space for individuals to share stories of kindness, raising awareness about the impact of compassion in various communities. This interconnectedness allows for the exchange of ideas and practices that can enhance kindness worldwide.

Practical Strategies to Promote Kindness in Society

Understanding the science behind kindness is crucial, but taking action to promote kindness in our communities is equally important. Here are some practical strategies to foster kindness on a larger scale:

1. **Organize Community Kindness Initiatives**: Work with local organizations to plan events that encourage acts of kindness, such as community clean-ups, food drives, or mentorship programs.

2. **Promote Kindness Education in Schools**: Advocate for programs in schools that teach children the importance of kindness and empathy. Educational institutions can play a pivotal role in shaping the values of future generations.

3. **Leverage Social Media for Kindness Campaigns**: Use social media platforms to share stories of kindness, inspiring others to participate in compassionate acts. Create hashtags that promote kindness initiatives, encouraging individuals to join the movement.

4. **Recognize and Celebrate Acts of Kindness**: Create opportunities to acknowledge and celebrate individuals who demonstrate kindness within your community. Public recognition can inspire others to engage in similar behaviors.

5. **Foster Intergenerational Connections**: Encourage interactions between different age groups to promote understanding and kindness. Programs that pair younger individuals with seniors can facilitate meaningful connections and a shared sense of community.

6. **Encourage Kindness in the Workplace**: Advocate for workplace initiatives that promote kindness, such as team-building activities centered around community service. Create an environment where employees feel empowered to engage in acts of kindness.

7. **Lead by Example**: Model kindness in your daily interactions, whether at home, work, or in public. By embodying the values of compassion and empathy, you can inspire those around you to do the same.

As we conclude our exploration of the science behind kindness, it's essential to recognize the profound effects that kindness can have on both individuals and society as a whole. The evidence is compelling: kindness not only enriches our mental and emotional well-being but also strengthens our connections with others, creating a web of compassion that binds us together.

In a world where stress and anxiety are increasingly common, embracing kindness is not just an act of goodwill; it's a powerful tool for improving our quality of life. The neurological and biological responses that occur when we engage in acts of kindness reinforce the notion that kindness is essential for our well-being. By reducing stress hormones and enhancing our emotional resilience, kindness becomes a critical component of a fulfilling and happy life.

Moreover, the transformative power of kindness extends far beyond individual benefits. It fosters strong relationships, cultivates community bonds, and promotes a culture of empathy and understanding. Whether through small daily gestures or large community initiatives, every act of kindness contributes to a more connected and compassionate world.

As we carry these insights into our daily lives, let us remember that kindness is not merely an abstract concept; it is a practical, actionable choice we can make every day. Each time we choose kindness, we are making a conscious decision to enhance our own lives and the lives of those around us.

So, as you move forward, consider how you can integrate kindness into your life. Whether it's through a simple smile, a helping hand, or a moment of understanding, each act creates ripples of positivity that can resonate far beyond what we can see. By actively choosing kindness, we not only improve our mental health but also contribute to a culture that values compassion and empathy.

In our next chapter, we will delve deeper into the superpower of kindness and how empathy can serve as a catalyst for meaningful change in our relationships and communities. We'll uncover stories of transformation, examine the narratives of those who have turned their lives around through kindness, and explore how we can harness this incredible power to uplift ourselves and others.

Let us embark on this journey together, embracing kindness as our guiding light and unlocking the potential within us all to make the world a better place—one act of kindness at a time.

CHAPTER FOUR

Everyday Kindness: Small Actions, Big Impact

In a fast-paced world filled with challenges and distractions, it can sometimes feel difficult to prioritize kindness. Yet, the reality is that kindness does not always require grand gestures; rather, it is often the small, consistent acts that create the most significant impact. This chapter will explore how to practice kindness even in tough times, share ideas for random acts of kindness in daily life, and provide steps to make kindness a lasting habit in your lifestyle.

How to Practice Kindness Even When Life Gets Tough

Life is full of challenges—stressful jobs, family issues, financial concerns, and global events can weigh heavily on our shoulders. During these tough times, it can be easy to retreat into ourselves, becoming overwhelmed by our problems and forgetting to extend kindness to others. However, it is precisely during these challenging moments that kindness becomes most crucial, not only for those around us but for our own mental health as well.

1. Start with Self-Kindness

Before you can extend kindness to others, it's vital to practice self-kindness. Acknowledge your feelings and give yourself grace during difficult times. Remember, it's okay to feel overwhelmed. Taking a moment to breathe, reflect, and forgive yourself for any perceived shortcomings can help you regain perspective. When you treat yourself with compassion, you are better equipped to share that kindness with others.

2. Acknowledge the People Around You

In tough times, it's common to become self-focused, but it's essential to remember that everyone is fighting their own battles. A simple acknowledgment of someone else's struggles can go a long way. For instance, if a colleague is having a rough day, a few encouraging words can uplift their spirit. Try to be mindful of the emotions and experiences of those around you, and respond with empathy.

3. Create a Kindness Checklist

When life feels overwhelming, it can help to have a go-to list of small acts of kindness you can engage in. This checklist can include simple actions like sending a text to check on a friend, complimenting a coworker, or even holding the door open for someone. When you consciously choose to perform one small act of kindness each day, it shifts your focus from your challenges to the positive impact you can make.

4. Embrace the Power of Listening

Sometimes, people just need someone to listen to them. Practicing active listening can be a profound act of kindness. When someone shares their struggles, take the time to truly hear them. Avoid the urge to jump in with advice or solutions unless asked; often, people just want to feel understood and validated.

5. Find a Supportive Community

Surrounding yourself with kind, supportive individuals can make a world of difference during tough times. Whether it's friends, family, or online groups, being part of a community that values kindness can help you stay motivated. When you see others practicing kindness, it inspires you to do the same, creating a cycle of compassion.

Random Acts of Kindness: Ideas for Everyday Life

Random acts of kindness are spontaneous gestures that can brighten someone's day. They require minimal planning and can often have a ripple effect, inspiring others to act kindly as well. Here are some practical ideas for infusing kindness into your daily life:

1. Write a Note of Appreciation

A heartfelt note can be a powerful way to show appreciation. Leave a thank-you note for a coworker, a loved one, or even a stranger who provided you with exceptional service. It costs nothing but can uplift someone's spirit significantly.

2. Share Your Skills

If you have a talent or skill that can help others—be it cooking, gardening, or even tutoring—offer your assistance. This not only helps others but also strengthens your community bonds and fosters connection.

3. Pay for Someone's Coffee

A classic example of a random act of kindness is paying for someone's coffee or meal. This gesture, no matter how small, can create a positive chain reaction, encouraging the recipient to pay it forward.

4. Leave Positive Comments Online

In the age of social media, kindness can be as simple as leaving encouraging comments on someone's post or sharing an uplifting article. Your positive words can make a big difference in someone's day.

5. Volunteer Your Time

Consider dedicating a few hours each month to volunteer in your community. Whether it's at a local shelter, animal rescue, or youth program, your time and effort can significantly impact those in need.

6. Smile and Make Eye Contact

Sometimes, the simplest act of kindness is a smile. It can break the ice, make someone feel seen, and even brighten their day. Smile at strangers, make eye contact, and engage in brief conversations whenever possible.

Building a Habit of Kindness: Making it a Lifestyle

Making kindness a consistent part of your life requires intention and practice. Here are some actionable steps to help you integrate kindness into your daily routine, transforming it into a lifelong habit:

1. Set Kindness Goals

Consider setting specific kindness goals for yourself. This could be committing to perform one act of kindness per day or volunteering once a month. Write these goals down and track your progress, celebrating small victories along the way.

2. Start a Kindness Journal

Keeping a journal dedicated to your acts of kindness can help reinforce the habit. Write about the kind things you did, how they made you feel, and the reactions of others. This reflection can motivate you to continue your efforts.

3. Share Your Journey

Share your experiences and commitment to kindness with others. Whether it's through social media, a blog, or simply sharing with friends, you can inspire those around you to join you on this journey. When you hold yourself accountable publicly, it becomes easier to stay committed.

4. Practice Gratitude

Incorporating gratitude into your life can enhance your kindness practice. Regularly take time to reflect on the positive aspects of your life and express gratitude for the people who support you. This mindset shift can lead to a greater desire to give back.

5. Be Open to Learning

Understanding that kindness can take many forms is essential to making it a lifelong habit. Be open to learning from different cultures, traditions, and perspectives about kindness. Engage with literature, attend workshops, or participate in community events that emphasize compassion and empathy. This exposure will broaden your understanding and enhance your ability to practice kindness in diverse situations.

6. Surround Yourself with Kindness

As mentioned earlier, the company you keep can significantly influence your behavior. Surround yourself with people who embody kindness. Their attitudes and actions can serve as inspiration, and you'll find that kindness becomes a natural part of your interactions. Additionally, consider participating in or starting kindness-focused groups or initiatives, which can further amplify your efforts.

7. Reflect and Adjust

Regularly take time to reflect on your kindness practices. Ask yourself: Are you being as kind as you want to be? Are there areas where you could improve? This reflection allows you to adjust your approach, ensuring that your efforts remain genuine and impactful. It can also serve as a reminder to keep kindness at the forefront of your daily life.

8. Celebrate Kindness

Celebrate your acts of kindness and those of others! Whether it's through a special gathering or a shout-out on social media, acknowledging kindness can foster a supportive environment. Share stories of kindness that you've experienced or witnessed; this not only reinforces your commitment but also spreads positivity throughout your network.

9. Make Kindness a Family Affair

Involve your family in your kindness journey. Encourage your children to participate in acts of kindness, creating a culture of compassion at home. This could include family volunteering days, crafting cards for the elderly, or simply sharing stories of kindness before bedtime. Teaching children about kindness from a young age ensures that they carry these values into adulthood.

10. Stay Committed to Kindness

Above all, commitment is crucial. There will be days when kindness feels challenging, especially during stressful or overwhelming times. However, remind yourself that kindness is a choice, and making that choice consistently, even when it's difficult, strengthens your ability to impact others positively.

As you continue to weave kindness into your daily life, you'll likely find that it becomes a natural part of who you are. The more you practice kindness, the more instinctive it becomes. You'll start to recognize opportunities for kindness everywhere, leading to a more compassionate outlook on life.

Embracing a Kindness Mindset

To truly integrate kindness into your lifestyle, it's essential to adopt a kindness mindset. This means viewing the world through a lens of compassion and recognizing that every interaction is an opportunity to make a difference. Here are some strategies to help cultivate this mindset:

1. Daily Kindness Affirmations

Start each day with a positive affirmation focused on kindness. Phrases like "I will spread kindness today" or "I choose compassion in every interaction" can set a powerful tone for your day. Repeat these affirmations during your morning routine or write them down in a journal. This practice reinforces your commitment and helps you stay mindful of your intention throughout the day.

2. Observe and Reflect

Make it a habit to observe acts of kindness around you. Whether it's a friend helping another, a stranger holding the door open, or someone offering a kind word, notice these moments and reflect on their impact. This practice can enhance your appreciation for kindness in the world, motivating you to contribute to that positivity.

3. Kindness Challenges

Participate in or create kindness challenges, either individually or within your community. These can be as simple as "30 Days of Kindness," where you commit to one act of kindness each day, or more elaborate challenges that encourage collective participation, like "Kindness Month" in schools or workplaces. Challenges can foster community spirit and make kindness a shared value.

4. Create Kindness Reminders

To keep kindness at the forefront of your mind, consider creating visual reminders. Post sticky notes with kind messages on your bathroom mirror, computer, or fridge. Set reminders on your phone with motivational quotes about kindness. These reminders can serve as nudges to act kindly, especially on days when you might feel stressed or overwhelmed.

5. Practice Forgiveness

Forgiveness is an integral part of kindness. Holding onto grudges can create emotional barriers, making it difficult to act kindly. Practice forgiveness by letting go of past grievances. This doesn't mean condoning harmful behavior but rather freeing yourself from the emotional burden of anger and resentment. When you forgive, you open your heart to kindness, not only toward others but also toward yourself.

Celebrating Acts of Kindness

As you incorporate kindness into your lifestyle, it's essential to celebrate not only your acts but also those of others. Celebrating kindness creates a positive feedback loop, encouraging more compassionate behavior.

1. Kindness Awards

If you're involved in a community or workplace, consider establishing kindness awards to recognize individuals who embody kindness in their actions. These awards can highlight the importance of kindness and motivate others to participate in similar behaviors. Celebrate the recipients publicly, reinforcing the value of kindness.

2. Share Stories of Kindness

Create a platform—be it a social media page, community bulletin board, or newsletter—dedicated to sharing stories of kindness. Encourage people to submit their experiences or highlight acts of kindness they've witnessed. By amplifying these stories, you inspire others to engage in kind actions and build a supportive community.

3. Host Kindness Events

Organize events that focus on kindness and community engagement. These could include community clean-up days, kindness fairs, or workshops centered around kindness skills like empathy and active listening. Such events provide an opportunity to foster connection and showcase the collective power of kindness.

4. Thank-You Notes Campaign

Encourage a thank-you notes campaign in schools, workplaces, or community organizations. This initiative can involve writing thank-you notes to individuals who have made a difference in your life or the community. Collect these notes and present them at a special event to celebrate kindness and express gratitude.

Building a Kindness Legacy

As you integrate kindness into your life, consider the legacy you wish to leave. A legacy of kindness can inspire future generations, creating a culture where compassion thrives.

1. Lead by Example

Your actions speak volumes. By consistently practicing kindness, you set a standard for those around you. Whether it's your family, friends, or coworkers, your commitment to kindness can inspire others to follow suit.

2. Teach Kindness

If you have children or mentor others, actively teach the principles of kindness. Share stories, engage in discussions, and create opportunities for them to practice kindness. Teaching kindness not only reinforces your values but also empowers others to make compassionate choices.

3. Document Your Journey

Consider documenting your kindness journey through writing or video. This record can serve as a testament to your commitment and can be shared with others to encourage them on their kindness paths. Reflecting on your growth can also help reinforce your dedication to this lifestyle.

4. Collaborate with Local Organizations

Partner with local nonprofits or community organizations that focus on kindness and compassion. These collaborations can amplify your impact, providing opportunities for larger-scale kindness initiatives that benefit the community.

5. Advocate for Kindness

Engage in conversations about kindness within your community. Advocate for policies or initiatives that promote compassion, whether it's through schools, workplaces, or local government. Your voice can help influence positive change and encourage a culture of kindness.

Kindness in the Workplace

Incorporating kindness into the workplace can significantly enhance team dynamics, improve morale, and increase productivity. A culture of kindness fosters collaboration, reduces stress, and creates an environment where individuals feel valued and appreciated. Here are several ways to cultivate kindness in a professional setting:

1. Lead with Kindness

Leadership plays a crucial role in establishing a culture of kindness within an organization. Leaders who prioritize kindness set a positive tone for the entire team. This can be achieved through simple gestures, such as expressing gratitude for employees' hard work, listening actively to their concerns, and being approachable. When leaders model kindness, it encourages employees to reciprocate those behaviors.

2. Create a Kindness Committee

Form a committee dedicated to promoting kindness within the workplace. This group can organize activities and initiatives focused on fostering compassion among employees. Some ideas include team-building exercises centered on kindness, recognition programs for employees who exemplify kind behavior, and brainstorming sessions for community service projects.

3. Encourage Open Communication

Establishing open lines of communication is vital in promoting a culture of kindness. Encourage team members to share their thoughts, ideas, and concerns without fear of judgment. Create safe spaces for discussions, where employees can express themselves honestly and support one another. This openness cultivates trust and strengthens relationships within the team.

4. Celebrate Achievements

Recognizing and celebrating achievements—both big and small—can create a positive atmosphere in the workplace. Whether it's a team milestone, a personal achievement, or a successful project completion, taking the time to celebrate fosters a sense of belonging and appreciation. You could organize monthly recognition events, where team members can share their successes and express gratitude toward one another.

5. Promote Work-Life Balance

Encouraging a healthy work-life balance is another essential aspect of kindness in the workplace. Support your colleagues in maintaining their well-being by respecting their boundaries and encouraging breaks. Offer flexible work arrangements, if possible, to help employees manage their responsibilities outside of work. When employees feel that their personal lives are valued, they are more likely to contribute positively to the workplace culture.

Acts of Kindness in Customer Interactions

The impact of kindness extends beyond internal workplace relationships; it also plays a significant role in customer interactions. Businesses that prioritize kindness in their customer service practices are more likely to build lasting relationships and cultivate loyal customers.

1. Personalize Customer Interactions

Take the time to personalize customer interactions by addressing individuals by their names and remembering their preferences. Simple gestures, like sending a handwritten thank-you note after a purchase or following up to ensure satisfaction, can leave a lasting impression. Customers appreciate feeling valued, and personalized interactions can enhance their overall experience.

2. Train Employees on Kindness in Customer Service

Invest in training programs that emphasize the importance of kindness in customer service. Equip employees with the skills and tools necessary to handle difficult situations with empathy and understanding. Role-playing scenarios can help employees practice responding to customer concerns with kindness, enabling them to resolve issues while maintaining a positive atmosphere.

3. Empower Employees to Go the Extra Mile

Encourage employees to take initiative in providing exceptional service. Empower them to make decisions that benefit the customer without needing approval from management. When employees feel confident in their ability to be kind and helpful, they are more likely to create memorable experiences for customers.

4. Share Positive Customer Feedback

Create a culture of sharing positive feedback among team members. Celebrate instances where employees have gone above and beyond for customers, highlighting the impact of their kindness. This practice not only motivates individuals but also reinforces the importance of kindness in customer interactions.

5. Implement a Kindness Policy

Consider implementing a kindness policy within your organization, outlining the importance of kindness in all aspects of business operations. This policy can serve as a guiding principle for employees, encouraging them to prioritize compassion and empathy in their interactions with customers and colleagues alike.

The Broader Impact of Kindness on Society

Kindness is not only a personal or workplace endeavor; it has the potential to transform entire communities and society as a whole. When kindness becomes a collective value, it can create a ripple effect that fosters compassion, understanding, and cooperation among diverse groups.

1. Community Engagement

Engaging in community service is one of the most effective ways to spread kindness beyond individual interactions. Encourage employees or individuals to volunteer together, whether at local shelters, food banks, or environmental clean-up efforts. These shared experiences can strengthen bonds, foster teamwork, and make a positive impact on the community.

2. Advocacy for Kindness Initiatives

Support or initiate kindness-focused initiatives within your community. This could involve organizing events, campaigns, or partnerships with local organizations to promote acts of kindness. For instance, establishing a "Kindness Week" can inspire community members to engage in kind actions, culminating in a day of celebration that recognizes individuals who embody kindness.

3. Education on Kindness

Promote kindness in educational institutions by integrating kindness curricula into schools. Teach students the importance of empathy, compassion, and kindness from a young age. This early education can instill lifelong values, encouraging future generations to prioritize kindness in their interactions.

4. Addressing Social Issues through Kindness

Kindness can be a powerful tool in addressing social issues such as homelessness, poverty, and mental health challenges. Support initiatives that focus on providing resources and assistance to those in need, showing that kindness is not just about small acts but also about advocating for systemic change.

5. Creating a Culture of Inclusivity

Kindness is essential in creating inclusive communities. Encourage individuals to be mindful of their words and actions, promoting understanding and acceptance of diverse backgrounds, cultures, and perspectives. A culture of inclusivity fosters kindness by allowing everyone to feel seen, heard, and valued.

The Role of Technology in Kindness

As we delve deeper into our daily lives, technology plays an increasingly prominent role. While it can sometimes create distance between individuals, it also offers unprecedented opportunities to spread kindness. From social media to instant messaging apps, here's how we can leverage technology to foster a kinder world.

1. Kindness on Social Media

Social media platforms have the potential to amplify acts of kindness on a global scale. Sharing stories of kindness can inspire others and create a culture of compassion. Use platforms like Instagram,

Twitter, and Facebook to showcase positive actions, share inspirational quotes, or highlight community service initiatives. Create hashtags such as **#KindnessMatters** or **#KindnessChallenge** to encourage others to participate and share their own stories. The ripple effect can be enormous; a single post can reach thousands and motivate them to act kindly.

2. Virtual Support Communities

Online forums and support groups provide an excellent platform for individuals to seek help and offer support. Whether through Reddit, Facebook groups, or dedicated kindness apps, these communities allow people to share their experiences, challenges, and stories of kindness. These virtual spaces can become safe havens for those in need, fostering a sense of belonging and connection. Encourage your audience to engage in these communities, share their stories, and extend their kindness to those who may be struggling.

3. Digital Kindness Challenges

Digital challenges can serve as fun and engaging ways to promote kindness. For instance, initiate a **30-Day Kindness Challenge** where participants commit to performing one act of kindness each day. Encourage individuals to document their experiences through photos or videos and share them online. This not only spreads kindness but also fosters accountability and community participation. You could even create a dedicated website or app where users can track their progress and share their stories, creating a virtual tapestry of kindness.

4. Using Apps for Kindness

In an age where we use apps for nearly everything, why not have an app dedicated to kindness? There are existing platforms designed to encourage acts of kindness, such as **Karma**, which allows users to perform and document kind acts. This app provides prompts for daily kindness, allowing users to engage with others and share their experiences. Developing or promoting such apps can significantly enhance the culture of kindness by making it easily accessible.

5. Spreading Kindness through Online Campaigns

Organizations and businesses can use technology to launch online kindness campaigns. These campaigns can range from fundraising for local charities to organizing virtual events aimed at promoting kindness. Encourage your audience to participate by sharing these campaigns on social media, donating, or volunteering their time. Highlighting these initiatives can inspire individuals to contribute to the cause, ultimately fostering a culture of kindness that extends beyond geographical boundaries.

The Challenges of Kindness in a Digital Age

While technology can enhance our ability to spread kindness, it also presents unique challenges. It's essential to navigate these challenges mindfully to ensure that kindness remains genuine and impactful.

1. The Anonymity of Online Interactions

The anonymity of the internet can sometimes lead to negative behaviors, including cyberbullying and trolling. This contrast can be disheartening, especially when one considers the potential for kindness online. It's crucial to educate individuals about the impact of their words and actions online. Promote campaigns that encourage respectful dialogue and discourage negativity. Remind people that behind every screen is a real person with feelings and emotions.

2. The Comparison Trap

Social media can create an environment where individuals feel pressured to compare their lives with those of others. This comparison often leads to feelings of inadequacy and negativity. It's essential to remind your audience that social media is often a highlight reel, not an accurate representation of reality. Encourage followers to focus on their own journeys, practicing kindness towards themselves first. Share resources on mental health and self-compassion to foster a supportive online community.

3. Overwhelm of Information

With the vast amount of information available online, it can be overwhelming to discern what is genuinely kind or impactful. Encourage your audience to be selective about the content they consume. Promote organizations or individuals who embody kindness and positivity, creating a curated list of resources that inspire action. This helps to drown out the noise of negativity and refocus attention on positive messages.

4. Disconnect in Real Life

While online interactions can be powerful, they should not replace face-to-face connections. Encourage individuals to balance their digital engagements with real-world kindness. Share tips on how to transition online interactions into offline acts of kindness. For instance, if someone has shared a heartwarming story online, suggest reaching out personally to check on them or offering support in person.

5. The Importance of Authenticity

In the pursuit of kindness, authenticity is crucial. Many individuals may feel pressured to engage in acts of kindness for social media validation rather than genuine compassion. Encourage people to be authentic in their kindness, reminding them that it's the intention behind the action that truly matters. Authentic kindness creates deeper connections and more significant impacts than performative gestures.

The Power of Kindness in Difficult Times

Throughout history, humanity has faced challenges—natural disasters, economic downturns, and global pandemics—that test our resolve and compassion. In these moments of adversity, kindness can be a beacon of hope and resilience. Here's how we can harness the power of kindness during difficult times.

1. Supporting One Another

During challenging periods, it's vital to come together as a community. Whether it's offering emotional support to a friend going through a tough time or organizing a neighborhood effort to assist those in need, the power of collective kindness can create a safety net for those struggling. Share stories of communities coming together to support one another, showcasing the strength that kindness can provide.

2. Mental Health Support

Challenging times can take a toll on mental health. Encourage your audience to check in on friends and loved ones, offering a listening ear or a helping hand. Provide resources for mental health support, including hotlines, therapy options, and community groups. Normalize conversations around mental health, emphasizing that seeking help is a sign of strength, not weakness.

3. Acts of Service

Encourage individuals to engage in acts of service during difficult times. This could include volunteering at local shelters, providing meals to those in need, or even offering to run errands for neighbors who may be struggling. These acts of service not only provide practical assistance but also foster a sense of purpose and connection.

4. Kindness in Grief

When facing loss or grief, kindness can be incredibly healing. Encourage individuals to reach out to those who have lost someone, offering condolences, support, or simply a listening ear. Share resources on grief support and emphasize the importance of acknowledging feelings and emotions during such times.

5. Advocacy for Change

Sometimes, the most significant acts of kindness come in the form of advocacy for change. Encourage individuals to support causes that resonate with them, whether it's fighting for social justice, climate change, or mental health awareness. Empower your audience to use their voices and platforms to advocate for kindness and understanding in society, promoting collective action for positive change.

In a world that often feels chaotic and overwhelming, the profound impact of everyday kindness cannot be overstated. The small actions we take, whether a warm smile to a stranger or a thoughtful message to a friend, can resonate deeply within our communities and ripple outward in ways we may never fully comprehend.

As we navigate through life's challenges, let us remember that kindness is a choice we can make every day. It requires little effort yet yields immense rewards—not only for those we help but also for ourselves. Practicing kindness can uplift our spirits, strengthen our relationships, and create a sense of belonging in a sometimes isolating world.

This chapter has explored various avenues for integrating kindness into our daily routines, highlighting the transformative power of empathy, the advantages of technology, and the importance of maintaining authenticity. We've examined how acts of kindness can serve as a balm during difficult times, providing support, solace, and strength to those who need it most.

As we move forward, let's commit to making kindness a habit rather than a fleeting thought. By creating a lifestyle that embraces compassion, we contribute to a culture where kindness is the norm and not the exception.

In the words of the famous poet Maya Angelou, "I've learned that people will forget what you said, people will forget what you did, but people will never forget how you made them feel." Let us strive to make others feel valued, respected, and loved through our everyday actions.

With this spirit of kindness in mind, we will now transition into the next chapter, where we will delve into the broader implications of kindness and explore how fostering a compassionate society can lead to profound changes in our communities and the world at large. Together, let's carry the torch of kindness forward, illuminating the path for ourselves and those around us.

CHAPTER FIVE

Kindness in a Digital World

In our hyper-connected society, where technology has become the cornerstone of communication, the concept of kindness has taken on new dimensions. Social media, messaging apps, and online forums have become the arenas where we interact, share, and express ourselves. In this chapter, we will explore how kindness can thrive in the digital landscape, highlighting the importance of spreading positivity, responding to negativity with compassion, and building online communities that foster inclusivity.

Spreading Positivity Online: How to Be a Digital Role Model

The digital world offers us a unique platform to reach others, share ideas, and inspire change. However, with this power comes the responsibility to be mindful of our online presence. Every post, comment, and share contributes to the digital ecosystem. Therefore, being a digital role model means consciously choosing to spread positivity and kindness.

To begin, we must first understand the power of our words. A simple compliment, an encouraging message, or a heartfelt expression of gratitude can resonate with others and brighten their day. Social media platforms like Instagram and Twitter can serve as vehicles for kindness; a well-timed message of support can uplift someone who may be struggling with self-doubt or anxiety.

Consider starting a gratitude challenge, encouraging your followers to express appreciation for the people in their lives. This initiative not only fosters a culture of gratitude but also inspires others to reflect on the positive aspects of their lives. Sharing uplifting quotes, personal stories of kindness, or highlighting acts of compassion within your community can create a ripple effect, motivating others to do the same.

Furthermore, being transparent about our struggles and challenges can humanize us in the eyes of our audience. When we share our vulnerabilities, it can create a space where others feel safe to express their feelings. This authenticity cultivates a sense of connection, reminding us that we are not alone in our experiences.

Dealing with Negativity and Hate: Responding with Kindness

Unfortunately, the digital world is not without its challenges. Negativity, hate speech, and trolling can easily overshadow the positive interactions we strive to foster. However, how we respond to negativity can significantly impact our digital environment.

When faced with harsh comments or online bullying, it can be tempting to retaliate with anger or sarcasm. Yet, this reaction only perpetuates the cycle of negativity. Instead, we can choose kindness as our response. This does not mean we should tolerate harmful behavior; rather, it involves addressing negativity with compassion and assertiveness.

For instance, when confronted with a negative comment, take a moment to breathe and assess the situation. Instead of reacting impulsively, consider responding with understanding. Acknowledge the person's feelings and offer a different perspective. You might say, "I understand you feel this way, but I believe there's value in looking at it from another angle." This approach not only diffuses the situation but also models a constructive way to handle disagreements.

Moreover, it's essential to protect your mental well-being. If negativity becomes overwhelming, it's okay to take a step back from social media. Curate your online space by unfollowing accounts that bring you down and surrounding yourself with positivity. This self-care is not selfish; it's necessary for maintaining a healthy relationship with technology.

Building an Online Community Rooted in Kindness

Creating an online community rooted in kindness requires intentional effort and ongoing commitment. The digital realm can often feel fragmented and isolating, but by fostering inclusivity and compassion, we can build connections that transcend geographical barriers.

Start by establishing clear values for your community. Whether it's a Facebook group, a Discord server, or an Instagram page, define what kindness looks like within that space. Set guidelines that encourage respectful dialogue, empathy, and support. Encourage members to celebrate each other's achievements, share their stories, and offer advice when needed.

Additionally, actively engage with your community members. Respond to comments, ask for feedback, and show appreciation for their contributions. Hosting virtual events, such as kindness challenges or live Q&A sessions, can create opportunities for members to connect in real-time. These interactions foster a sense of belonging and create lasting relationships.

Highlight and recognize acts of kindness within your community. Feature members who exemplify kindness in their actions, whether through volunteering, supporting others, or sharing uplifting content. This recognition not only validates their efforts but also inspires others to contribute positively.

As we delve deeper into the digital landscape, it becomes increasingly clear that the role of kindness extends beyond mere interactions. It shapes the very culture of our online environments. The choices we make in how we communicate and connect can either contribute to a toxic atmosphere or foster a supportive community.

Navigating the Complexities of Online Interactions

Navigating the complexities of online interactions can be a challenge. Each comment and post represents not just words but also a connection to others' feelings and experiences. When we engage online, it's crucial to remember that there is a real person behind each profile—someone who has their own struggles, joys, and experiences.

This understanding should inform our online behavior. For example, when we see a post that triggers us—whether due to disagreement or misunderstanding—taking a moment to reflect before responding can be invaluable. Instead of jumping to conclusions or reacting impulsively, we can pause to ask ourselves how our response will impact the other person. Will it add to the conversation constructively, or will it contribute to division and hurt?

Engaging in active listening is also an essential skill in the digital world. This means taking the time to truly understand what someone is saying before forming a response. When we practice active listening online, we validate others' feelings and show that we value their perspectives. This, in turn, encourages a more respectful and understanding discourse, leading to a healthier online environment.

Encouraging Kindness in Digital Spaces

While we have the power to model kindness, we also have the ability to encourage others to join us in this mission. One effective strategy is to use our platforms to showcase examples of kindness. Sharing stories about individuals or organizations making a positive impact in their communities can inspire others to take action. Whether it's highlighting a local charity's work or recognizing someone's small act of kindness, these narratives can create a ripple effect, prompting others to reflect on their own potential for kindness.

Additionally, initiating campaigns or challenges centered around kindness can galvanize your audience. For instance, creating a "30 Days of Kindness" challenge on social media encourages followers to commit to one kind act each day for a month. Participants can share their experiences, creating a sense of community and shared purpose. Not only does this spread positivity, but it also inspires creativity in how we can be kind to one another.

Furthermore, consider utilizing hashtags to unify efforts. Hashtags like **#KindnessMatters** or **#ActsOfKindness** can help gather a collective voice, showcasing the overwhelming presence of kindness in our digital spaces. As more people engage with these hashtags, they become part of a larger movement that encourages a culture of compassion and understanding.

Promoting Digital Literacy and Empathy

As we navigate the complexities of the digital landscape, promoting digital literacy becomes essential. Understanding how to communicate effectively and respectfully online can significantly influence the quality of our interactions. Digital literacy encompasses not just the technical skills of using technology but also the social and emotional skills necessary for positive engagement.

Encouraging empathy in our online interactions starts with education. It is crucial to teach both children and adults about the impact of their words and actions in the digital world. Workshops, webinars, or even simple discussions about online etiquette and kindness can empower individuals to think critically about their online presence.

Moreover, creating content that focuses on empathy—such as articles, videos, or podcasts—can reach a wider audience. Topics could include how to handle online conflicts with grace, understanding diverse perspectives, and cultivating compassion in digital interactions.

By normalizing discussions around empathy and kindness, we can gradually shift the culture of online communication toward one that is more supportive and understanding.

Building Resilience Through Kindness

In addition to spreading kindness, we must also consider how acts of kindness can help build resilience. The digital world can sometimes be overwhelming, filled with negativity and challenges. However, engaging in kind acts—both for ourselves and others—can serve as a buffer against the stressors we encounter online.

For instance, practicing self-kindness, such as taking breaks from social media or engaging in mindfulness activities, is crucial for maintaining mental health. When we prioritize our well-being, we are better equipped to extend kindness to others. This self-care practice not only benefits us but also positively influences those around us.

Moreover, when we witness or engage in acts of kindness, our brains release oxytocin and dopamine—chemicals that promote feelings of happiness and connection. This creates a positive feedback loop; the more we practice kindness, the more we experience its benefits, reinforcing our commitment to fostering a kind digital environment.

Collective Action: The Future of Kindness in Digital Spaces

Looking ahead, the future of kindness in digital spaces relies on collective action. As individuals, we can commit to embodying kindness in our online interactions. However, creating systemic change requires collaboration among users, platforms, and organizations.

Social media platforms have a role to play in this evolution. By implementing features that promote positive engagement—such as kindness reminders, community guidelines focused on respect, and systems for reporting negativity—these platforms can help cultivate environments where kindness flourishes.

Additionally, businesses and organizations can contribute by developing campaigns that emphasize corporate social responsibility. By aligning with causes that promote kindness and inclusivity, they can harness their influence to create positive change in the digital realm.

As we further explore kindness in the digital realm, we find ourselves at a pivotal intersection of technology, communication, and human connection. With the rise of social media, instant messaging, and online forums, our world has become more interconnected than ever. However, this connectivity comes with its own set of challenges, necessitating a deeper understanding of how we can wield kindness as a powerful tool for positive change.

The Importance of Intentionality in Online Kindness

To cultivate kindness in digital spaces, we must prioritize intentionality in our online interactions. Intentionality means being deliberate about the messages we send, the comments we leave, and the content we share. It requires us to pause and reflect on the potential impact of our words before hitting "send" or "post."

One way to foster intentionality is through mindfulness practices. When we approach our online interactions with a mindful mindset, we become more aware of our emotions and reactions. This awareness allows us to respond to others with empathy rather than defensiveness, creating a more harmonious digital atmosphere.

For example, if someone shares a personal story of struggle or vulnerability, instead of hastily reacting with judgment or criticism, we can take a moment to empathize with their experience. Responding with kindness can validate their feelings and offer support, showing them that they are not alone in their challenges. Such interactions can be transformative, reinforcing the notion that the digital world can be a safe space for sharing and connecting.

Creating Safe Spaces for Dialogue

In the quest to spread kindness online, creating safe spaces for dialogue is essential. These spaces allow individuals to share their thoughts and feelings without fear of judgment or backlash. When people feel safe, they are more likely to express themselves authentically, leading to richer conversations and deeper connections.

Safe spaces can take various forms, such as online support groups, forums, or community platforms dedicated to specific interests or causes. For instance, mental health support groups on social media provide a refuge for individuals to share their experiences, seek advice, and connect with others who understand their struggles. By fostering an environment of kindness, these groups help break down stigma and promote open conversations about mental health.

Additionally, businesses and organizations can play a significant role in creating safe online environments. Implementing community guidelines that emphasize respect and kindness, alongside moderation policies that address bullying and harassment, can help maintain a culture of support and inclusivity.

The Role of Influencers and Content Creators

Influencers and content creators hold substantial power in shaping online culture. Their platforms allow them to reach vast audiences, making them ideal advocates for kindness. By consciously choosing to promote positive messages and share stories of compassion, they can inspire their followers to engage in similar behavior.

For instance, consider the impact of social media challenges that encourage acts of kindness. Influencers who participate in or initiate these challenges can mobilize their audience to take action. Whether it's promoting random acts of kindness, supporting charitable causes, or sharing uplifting stories, these influencers can amplify the message of kindness, creating a viral movement of compassion.

Moreover, the content shared by influencers can also help counteract negativity. For instance, when faced with a wave of online hate, influencers can respond by sharing positive affirmations, stories of resilience, or messages of unity. By doing so, they not only uplift their followers but also set an example of how to handle negativity with grace and positivity.

Empathy in the Age of Misinformation

In today's digital landscape, misinformation poses a significant challenge to kindness and empathy. With the rapid spread of false information, misunderstandings and conflicts can easily arise. In these situations, it's crucial to approach discussions with empathy and a willingness to listen.

When encountering misinformation or opposing viewpoints, instead of reacting with anger or dismissal, we can strive to engage in constructive dialogue. This means asking questions to better understand the other person's perspective, sharing reliable information calmly, and seeking common ground. By approaching these conversations with kindness, we not only promote better understanding but also model healthy communication practices.

Furthermore, as consumers of information, we can foster a culture of critical thinking and empathy by sharing credible sources and fact-checking information before spreading it. By doing so, we contribute to a more informed digital environment that values truth and understanding over sensationalism and division.

Harnessing the Power of Technology for Kindness

Technology itself can be harnessed to promote kindness in various innovative ways. For instance, apps that encourage gratitude and positive interactions can help individuals cultivate a mindset focused on appreciation and kindness. These apps may prompt users to share their acts of kindness or express gratitude toward others, creating a ripple effect of positivity.

Additionally, gamifying acts of kindness through apps or online platforms can motivate individuals to engage in kind behavior. For instance, a mobile app could reward users for completing acts of kindness, creating a fun and interactive way to spread goodwill. By incorporating elements of play, we can inspire people to embrace kindness as a regular part of their lives.

Moreover, digital platforms can be utilized for collaborative projects that emphasize kindness. Initiatives such as virtual volunteering or crowd-sourced kindness campaigns can mobilize communities to work together toward a common goal. By collaborating with others online, we can amplify our impact and foster a sense of belonging and shared purpose.

The Future of Kindness in Digital Spaces

As we look toward the future, it is evident that kindness will remain a vital component of our online interactions. The evolution of technology and social media will continue to shape how we connect and communicate. However, the choice to prioritize kindness lies within each of us.

Ultimately, the future of kindness in digital spaces will depend on our collective commitment to fostering empathy, compassion, and respect. By actively choosing to engage in positive interactions, create safe spaces, and counter negativity with kindness, we can build a digital landscape that reflects the best of humanity.

As we delve deeper into the complexities of kindness in our digital age, we must confront the various platforms that shape our interactions and the unique challenges they present. The rapid evolution of technology influences how we express ourselves, connect with others, and respond to the world around us. By examining the intricacies of our digital interactions, we can better understand how to cultivate a culture of kindness online.

The Dilemma of Anonymity

One of the defining features of the digital world is anonymity. While it can provide a sense of security, allowing people to express themselves without fear of judgment, it often leads to negative behaviors. Online anonymity can embolden individuals to engage in harmful actions, such as cyberbullying, trolling, and spreading misinformation. This dark side of anonymity can erode the foundations of kindness, making it essential for us to find ways to counteract this phenomenon.

To foster kindness in anonymous spaces, we must create and promote a culture of accountability. Encouraging individuals to take responsibility for their words and actions, regardless of whether their identities are revealed, can help mitigate harmful behavior. For instance, platforms can implement features that discourage toxic interactions, such as real-time moderation, reporting tools, and community guidelines that emphasize respectful communication.

Moreover, promoting positive anonymity can create safe spaces for vulnerable populations. For example, support groups for mental health or LGBTQ+ communities often rely on anonymity to provide a secure environment where individuals can share their experiences and seek support without fear of discrimination. By highlighting the positive aspects of anonymity, we can encourage people to use their digital presence to uplift and support one another.

Nurturing Digital Empathy

To combat the challenges posed by the digital landscape, nurturing empathy becomes crucial. Empathy allows us to step into someone else's shoes, fostering understanding and connection. Digital empathy involves not only understanding another person's feelings but also responding to them with kindness and compassion.

One effective way to promote digital empathy is through storytelling. When we share our personal experiences or listen to the stories of others, we create opportunities for connection and understanding. Storytelling humanizes our interactions and helps us recognize our shared humanity. For instance, social media platforms can host campaigns encouraging users to share their stories of struggle and triumph, promoting a culture of vulnerability and empathy.

Another powerful tool for nurturing digital empathy is education. By raising awareness about the impact of our words and actions online, we can cultivate a generation of compassionate digital citizens. Schools and organizations can implement programs that teach digital literacy and empathy, equipping individuals with the skills to navigate the online world with kindness. Workshops, seminars, and online courses focused on empathy-building can empower individuals to engage in thoughtful and respectful interactions.

The Role of Community in Digital Kindness

Communities play a pivotal role in shaping our online behavior. Whether we're part of a social media group, a forum, or a gaming community, the collective mindset of these spaces influences how we

practice can help us cultivate a habit of kindness, ensuring that our online interactions align with our values.

Moreover, digital detoxes can serve as valuable opportunities for reflection and self-care. Stepping away from screens allows us to reconnect with ourselves and those around us. During these breaks, we can engage in activities that promote kindness, whether through volunteering, connecting with loved ones, or practicing self-compassion.

Amplifying Kindness through Digital Storytelling

Digital storytelling is a powerful medium for spreading kindness and fostering empathy. By sharing our experiences and the experiences of others, we can create narratives that resonate with audiences and inspire positive change.

Platforms like YouTube, podcasts, and blogs offer spaces for individuals to tell their stories, highlighting acts of kindness that have made a difference in their lives. These narratives humanize the abstract concept of kindness, allowing listeners to connect emotionally with the experiences shared.

Moreover, collaborative storytelling initiatives can amplify the impact of individual narratives. For instance, creating a community project where participants share their kindness stories can foster a sense of unity and purpose. By bringing together diverse voices, we can create a rich tapestry of experiences that highlight the transformative power of kindness.

The Role of Influencers and Digital Leaders

Influencers and digital leaders have a unique opportunity to model kindness in their online presence. With large followings and significant reach, these individuals can inspire millions to engage in acts of kindness. By using their platforms to promote positive messages, they can drive meaningful change in their communities.

For instance, influencers can share their personal experiences with kindness, showcasing how it has impacted their lives and the lives of others. They can also collaborate with charitable organizations to raise awareness and funds for causes that promote kindness and compassion.

Additionally, influencers can create challenges or campaigns encouraging their followers to engage in acts of kindness. These initiatives can take various forms, from random acts of kindness challenges to community service days. By harnessing the power of social media, influencers can motivate their audiences to embrace kindness as a fundamental value.

Embracing Kindness in Online Discourse

In the digital world, discussions can quickly escalate into heated debates, often leading to hostility and division. Embracing kindness in online discourse is essential for fostering constructive conversations and maintaining healthy interactions.

One way to promote kindness in discussions is to prioritize active listening. When engaging in conversations, we can approach differing opinions with an open mind, seeking to understand the perspectives of others. This involves refraining from interrupting and allowing others to express their thoughts fully before responding.

Moreover, expressing gratitude can be a powerful tool in online interactions. Thanking individuals for sharing their viewpoints, even when we disagree, can help create a more respectful and positive atmosphere. Acknowledging the effort others put into sharing their opinions fosters a sense of community and encourages ongoing dialogue.

Additionally, using inclusive language can promote kindness in our discussions. Being mindful of our word choices can help create an environment where individuals feel valued and respected. This involves avoiding derogatory terms or dismissive phrases and instead opting for language that promotes understanding and connection.

The Future of Kindness in a Digital World

As we look toward the future, the role of kindness in our digital world will continue to evolve. Technology will undoubtedly advance, and our interactions will adapt to these changes. However, the fundamental principles of kindness will remain essential in navigating these shifts.

To ensure kindness remains at the forefront of our digital interactions, we must advocate for policies that promote online safety and respect. This includes supporting initiatives that combat cyberbullying, hate speech, and misinformation. By standing together as a community, we can hold platforms accountable for creating spaces that prioritize kindness and compassion.

Moreover, as new technologies emerge, we must consider how they can be leveraged to promote kindness. Innovations such as virtual reality and augmented reality can offer unique opportunities for empathy-building and connection. By embracing these technologies, we can find new ways to share kindness across boundaries and foster understanding in an increasingly complex world.

As we reach the end of this chapter, it's crucial to recognize that kindness in the digital world is not merely a choice but a responsibility we all share. In a landscape that can often seem divisive and overwhelming, our commitment to kindness serves as a guiding light, illuminating the path toward more meaningful connections and a more compassionate society.

By embracing kindness online, we not only enhance our personal experiences but also contribute to a broader cultural shift that prioritizes empathy and understanding. Each tweet, comment, or post has the potential to inspire others, create a sense of community, and foster relationships rooted in respect. Therefore, let us strive to be intentional in our digital interactions, remembering that our words and actions can resonate far beyond our screens.

As we move forward, let us take the lessons learned from this chapter and apply them in our everyday lives. Let's cultivate an online presence that reflects our values, advocates for positivity, and inspires others to do the same. Whether through simple acts of kindness or powerful advocacy, each of us can play a vital role in creating a digital environment where compassion reigns supreme.

Final Thoughts: The Journey of Kindness

As we conclude this book, *Kindness Costs Nothing, Yet It's Priceless*, we reflect on the profound impact kindness can have on our lives, relationships, and communities. Each chapter has explored different facets of kindness, illustrating that it is not a fleeting sentiment but a powerful force that can transform our world.

Kindness is a journey, one that begins with small, intentional actions and expands into larger movements that challenge the status quo. From the ripple effect of a single kind gesture to the collective impact of a community dedicated to compassion, every act of kindness contributes to a more just and loving world.

Let us carry the principles of kindness with us as we navigate our lives. In our homes, workplaces, and communities, let us be advocates for kindness, embracing empathy, understanding, and respect in every interaction. Together, we can create a legacy of kindness that inspires future generations to continue this vital work.

In closing, remember that kindness is a gift that costs nothing yet enriches our lives immeasurably. May we all choose to be vessels of kindness, spreading joy, compassion, and hope wherever we go. Thank you for joining me on this journey, and may your path be filled with kindness and warmth.

Thank You

Milton Keynes UK
Ingram Content Group UK Ltd.
UKHW032035191024
449814UK00010B/518